THE GROOVY SIDE OF THE '60s

Writers: Tom DeMichael and Rhonda Markowitz

Publications International, Ltd.

Tom DeMichael is coauthor of *The Best American History Quiz Book* as well as the author of *Love Those Stooges: Trivia Challenge and Reference Guide*. He has also written numerous articles on American cinema.

Rhonda Markowitz is the author of *Folk, Pop, Mods and Rockers: The British Invasion 1960–1966*. As a senior writer for MTV News, she received a Peabody Award. Her work has also appeared on VH1 and in *Tracks* and other magazines.

Factual verification by **Regina Montgomery**.

Acknowledgments:

"Vega 200" by Victor Vasarely. Copyright © 2005 Artists Rights Society (ARS), New York/ADAGP, Paris. Reprinted with permission.

"Campbell's Black Bean Soup" by Andy Warhol. Copyright © 2005 Andy Warhol Foundation for the Visual Arts/ARS, New York/™Licensed by Campbell's Soup Co. All rights reserved. Reprinted with permission.

"Reverie from the Portfolio of 11 Pop Artists" by Roy Lichtenstein. Copyright © Estate of Roy Lichtenstein. Reprinted with permission.

Contents

Chapter 1

The Times They Are a-Changin'

Bob Dylan wrote and recorded "The Times They Are a-Changin'" in 1963. It appeared on his album of the same name.

Former WWII hero Dwight D. "Ike" Eisenhower possessed personal popularity, an unbeatable nickname, and a devoted and well-loved wife, Mamie, while he led America to unprecedented peace and prosperity during two terms in the White House (1953–1961). A moderate Republican, Ike expanded Social Security, increased the minimum wage to $1.00 an hour, and tried to reduce Cold War tensions abroad and address civil rights controversies at home. Life seemed good as the new decade dawned.

With the addition of Alaska and Hawaii as U.S. states in 1959—the first expansion of the union in almost 50 years—a new version of the **Stars and Stripes** was in order to replace the old 48-star model. The new flag with the 50-star field was officially flown for the first time on July 4, 1960.

The **Pittsburgh Pirates** became baseball's world champions in the seven-game 1960 World Series against the New York Yankees. Many baseball historians name Game 7 of the series as the most dramatic ever played. The Pirates rallied in the bottom of the eighth inning, scoring five and taking a 9–7 lead. The Yanks tied it up in the ninth in amazing fashion, potentially forcing extra innings. But Pittsburgh second baseman Bill Maze-roski, leading off in

the bottom of the ninth, smashed a climactic game-winning homer that brought the players and Pittsburgh fans to their feet. Jubilant fans poured onto the field to celebrate the first World Series–ending homer in history.

Detroit continued to make large, heavy-duty cars. Lincolns were styled to look big—and they *were* big, at more than 19 feet bumper to bumper. In 1960, the average family earned $5,600—the Lincoln Continental Mark V convertible cost $7,056. Cadillacs continued to come with tailfins. But change was in the air, as the big three automakers introduced compact cars such as the Ford Falcon, the Chevy Corvair, and the Valiant from Chrysler. The Edsel took its last lap around the lot and was discontinued in 1960.

Clockwise from top right: *1960 Cadillac Eldorado; 1960 Lincoln Continental Mark V; 1960 Ford Falcon; 1960 Chevrolet Corvair*

Dick Clark Plays the Hits

Dick Clark broadcast from Philadelphia and introduced his young audience to teen idols such as **Frankie Avalon, Fabian, Bobby Rydell,** Paul Anka, and Ricky Nelson (whose parents, Ozzie and Harriet, had their own sitcom). The

kids who were *American Bandstand*'s regular dancers became almost as famous as the music stars when they rated records or demonstrated the latest dance steps. Clark insisted on racial diversity in both the in-studio crowd and performers, giving early breaks to Little Richard, Chuck Berry, Chubby Checker, James Brown, Marvin Gaye, and Smokey Robinson and the Miracles.

After **Chubby Checker** (whose name was a takeoff on Fats Domino) performed "The Twist" on *American Bandstand* in 1960, it became an international dance craze. Instructions were simple: Act like you're stubbing out a cigarette while you dry your back with a towel.

A-vun, an' A-two

Bandleader **Lawrence Welk** never quite lost his Germanic accent, but that didn't prevent him from becoming one of America's most popular TV hosts. For three decades he remained a comfort to older audiences who hated what they thought of as the caterwauling that now passed as music.

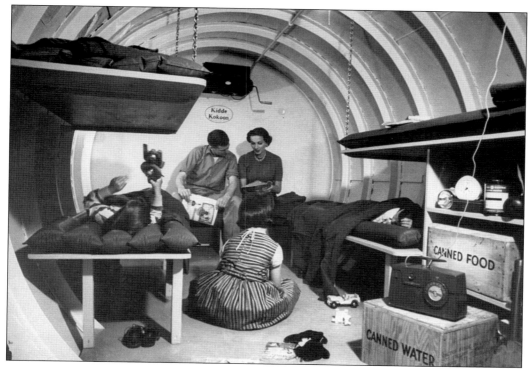

The ever-present fear of nuclear war led many Americans to consider building **fallout shelters** in their backyards. Supposedly **"bomb-proof,"** these reinforced holes in the ground pretended to offer protection for up to two weeks. Some were simply plywood and sand; others, elaborate structures of steel and reinforced concrete. All would theoretically save you and your family in the event of a nuclear strike.

The Beat Generation

Who belonged to the "Beat Generation"? Young writers, free from the manacles that the established literary world tried to fasten on their wrists. Untamed and reckless, the Beats tackled topics and images in a stream of consciousness that reflected a different slant on America. They wrote of emancipation—social, sexual, and spiritual. They traveled the country by hitching rides and hopping freight trains.

IMPORTANT BEAT WORKS

◀ *Howl and Other Poems*, Allen Ginsberg

A Coney Island of the Mind, Lawrence Ferlinghetti

On the Road, Jack Kerouac

Preface to a Twenty Volume Suicide Note, LeRoi Jones

One Flew Over the Cuckoo's Nest, Ken Kesey

Trout Fishing in America, Richard Brautigan

Naked Lunch, William S. Burroughs ▲

A Confederate General from Big Sur, Richard Brautigan

Poems for Freddie, Diane DiPrima

Big Sur, Jack Kerouac

Dutchman, LeRoi Jones

In 1961 not one but *two* men were in full rush to bust Babe Ruth's single-season home run record—Yankee sluggers **Mickey Mantle** and **Roger Maris**. While New York's fans and reporters didn't mind if the charismatic Mantle broke the record, they gave Maris a hard time. By late August, injuries had knocked Mantle off the pace, and he finished the season with 54 homers. Despite insomnia and nightmares, Maris persevered. In the season's final game, he belted No. 61 against Boston in Yankee Stadium.

From tee to green, no other golfers in the '60s could mesmerize a gallery like **Arnold Palmer** and Jack Nicklaus. Palmer, whose fans were known as "Arnie's Army," seemed unstoppable in the early years of the decade. Nicklaus, however, known as "The Golden Bear," proved a match for Palmer. He was the PGA Player of the Year in 1967, a feat Palmer had accomplished in 1960 and 1962.

Sitcoms were abundant on '60s TV. Andy Griffith played good-natured Sheriff Andy Taylor in *The Andy Griffith Show*, a situation comedy that always ranked high in the ratings. With Don Knotts as Deputy Barney Fife, he maintained order in the rather peaceful hamlet of Mayberry, North Carolina. The show's whistled theme song became a favorite of baby boomers.

Kennedy Faces Off Against Nixon

Watched by an estimated 66.4 million viewers in 1960, Massachusetts Senator John F. Kennedy faced off against Vice President Richard Nixon in the first-ever presidential TV debate. The senator looked youthful, tanned, and immaculately dressed. Nixon, on the other hand, appeared drawn, having just spent two weeks in the hospital for a knee injury. He would have been well advised to use makeup to cover up his perspiration and five o'clock shadow. For many in the TV audience, it was like watching a vibrant leader versus a washed-out salesperson.

"Let the word go forth from this time and place, to friend and foe alike, that the torch has been passed to a new generation of Americans."

"My fellow Americans: ask not what your country can do for you—ask what you can do for your country. My fellow citizens of the world: ask not what America will do for you, but what together we can do for the freedom of man."

John F. Kennedy, Inaugural Address, January 20, 1961

New heroes emerged at the 1960 Olympic Games in Rome. American sprinter Wilma Rudolph, diagnosed with polio as a child, overcame her disease and won three gold medals: in the 100- and 200-meter dashes and as a member of the 400-meter relay team. Rafer Johnson set a new Olympic record in the decathlon. And a new face was introduced to American boxing when Cassius Clay won the light-heavyweight gold medal.

"And That's the Way It Is"

It was an evening tradition by now for Americans to get their news from the avuncular Walter Cronkite on CBS—whose exit line was "And that's the way it is"—or the NBC team of Chet Huntley, based in New York, and David Brinkley in Washington, who had their own snappy closing. At the end of each broadcast, after speaking only to viewers until then, the anchors would address each other to say farewell. "Good night, Chet." "Good night, David. And good night for NBC News." Brinkley was never comfortable with the concept, thinking the move was grandstanding that took away from the news itself.

News was also circulated in other ways. Millions of adolescent boys would rise before dawn to get on their bikes and deliver newspapers to suburban front doors or damp lawns. Girls often earned their spending money by babysitting.

If the Shoe Hits...

"The Cold War" referred to the conflict between the superpowers of the United States of America and the Union of Soviet Socialist Republics,

or Russia. In some ways it was a clash of ideologies between capitalism and communism, but in others it was a struggle for power and influence over the rest of the world. By the 1960s, both sides had developed nuclear weapons, and the Communist threat hung over Americans like the sword of Damocles. On a trip to New York, Soviet Premier Nikita Khrushchev was reported to have banged his shoe on the desk as a way of getting the UN General Assembly's attention in October 1960.

Drive-in movies, first launched in the '30s, soared in popularity. As the '60s began, there were more than 5,000 drive-in theaters throughout the country. They offered families the chance to see a film with the kids already in their pajamas. But they're perhaps more infamously remembered for the opportunities they provided teenagers to "neck" in privacy.

Movie tickets cost less than a dollar.

The First Lady Brings Elegance to the White House

Jacqueline Bouvier Kennedy had grown up in the upper class on New York's Long Island and near the nation's capital. Wasting no time in sharing her keen appreciation of the finer things in life with the White House and the country, the First Lady influenced a generation. Her sharp sense of fashion led to worldwide trends in pillbox hats and tailored Oleg Cassini suits, and her exquisite taste in decorating and entertaining, along with her well-crafted public image, touched people around the globe. When JFK and Jackie traveled the world, the First Lady often attracted as many admirers as the President.

Caroline and John-John

The White House had seldom seen anything like it. First Families did not usually include toddlers and infants. But there was nothing "usual" about the youthful Jack and Jackie Kennedy. Their daughter, Caroline, was just three years old when Daddy was elected to the presidency in 1960. **John, Jr.,** was born only a few weeks after the election. Sadly, a third child named Patrick Bouvier was born prematurely and died only two days after his birth in August 1963.

Barbie's Dream Life

The first Barbie doll sported a blonde ponytail, a stylish black-and-white zebra-stripe bathing suit, open-toe shoes, sunglasses, and earrings, not to mention measurements (38–18–34) that would have made Jayne Mansfield envious.

In 1961, the fictional Barbie (full name Barbara Millicent Roberts) was a teenage fashion model from Willow High School, where she would meet her boyfriend (and follow-up doll), Ken Carson.

Hot Toys

Mr. Machine

Slinky

Rock 'Em Sock 'Em Robots

Chatty Cathy Doll

Silly Putty

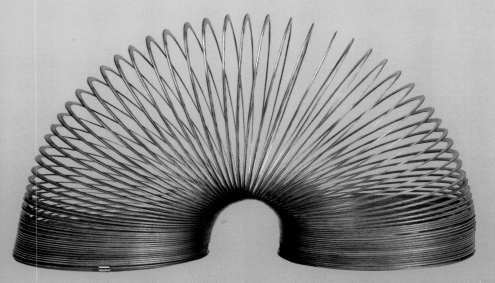

Influential Books of the Era

To Kill A Mockingbird, Harper Lee

The Fire Next Time, James Baldwin

The Feminine Mystique, Betty Friedan

Black Like Me, John Howard Griffin

Profiles in Courage, John F. Kennedy

A Clockwork Orange, Anthony Burgess

The Rise and Fall of the Third Reich, William L. Shirer

Sex and the Single Girl, Helen Gurley Brown

Silent Spring, Rachel Carson

Catch–22, Joseph Heller

The Bell Jar, Sylvia Plath

Rabbit, Run, John Updike

Green Eggs and Ham, Dr. Seuss

Where the Wild Things Are, Maurice Sendak

One Flew Over the Cuckoo's Nest, Ken Kesey

The Pill

Birth control became easily available through "the Pill." A tablet of synthetic hormones that prevented conception, it needed no further identification or explanation—everyone knew what "the Pill" meant. By 1968, almost 16 million women were using the Pill, seen as the key to sexual freedom.

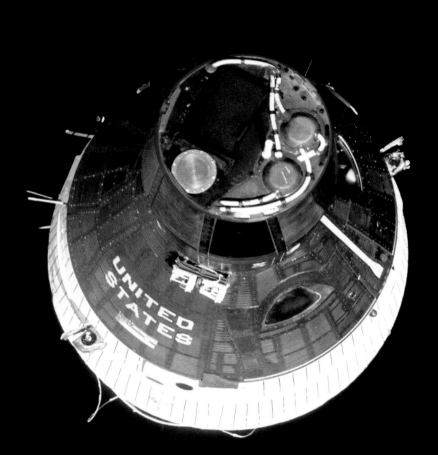

The Space Race

Russia astounded the world by launching a satellite called *Sputnik* into orbit around Earth in late 1957. While it was designed to perform scientific measurements, the implications were clear—advantage in the Cold War was Russia's real motivation for reaching outer space. The United States responded by successfully launching its first satellite, *Explorer 1*, in 1958. The Space Race was off and running.

In the '60s, the Russians again struck first by placing cosmonaut Yuri Gagarin into orbit in early 1961. America answered by launching **Alan Shepherd** into space a month later. His *Freedom 7* Mercury spacecraft soared into space on a not-as-impressive suborbital flight. In less than a year, John Glenn rode his *Friendship 7* spacecraft into space, becoming the first American to orbit Earth.

By the time of the first two-astronaut **Gemini** flight in 1965, America was beginning to nose the Russians out of the lead in the Race for Space.

World's Fair in Seattle

Running for exactly six months in 1962, the Seattle World's Fair hosted 24 nations from around the world and saw an average of 20,000 visitors a day, with total attendance reaching more than 9.5 million people. Nicknamed "The Century 21 Exposition," the fair offered its take on the world of science in the future.

The centerpiece of the World's Fair was the astonishing spire of steel and glass called the Space Needle. At 605 feet tall, it was constructed at a cost of $4.5 million. Brainchild of World's Fair Commissioner Eddie Carlson, the concept of the Space Needle had originally been sketched quickly on a placemat. Architect John Graham fleshed out the design, essentially a flying saucer on a tripod, which would contain a revolving restaurant and observation deck offering spectacular sights for diners and visitors alike.

The 21st century had arrived 38 years early in Seattle.

SEATTLE WORLD'S FAIR 1962

It's April 21, 1962, in Seattle...World's Fair time! The curtain's going up on the 21st Century...and on the most exciting preview ever seen. This is Seattle's spectacular Space-Age World's Fair, where the epic of man's journey into the next 100 years will unfold for you. What's ahead? How will man live? What will he see? Look at cities in the year 2000, see homes whose walls are jets of air, where cordless appliances work for you, cars ride without wheels, TV wrist telephones speed everyday communications. Time and distance will disappear in the gigantic, pillar-less Coliseum Century 21, jutting eleven stories up from the heart of the fair. You'll soar past the moon into outer galaxies—no space suit, no gravity, in the $9 million complex of the United States Science Pavilion. You will discover the secrets of the future in these six gleaming buildings rising above lighted fountains and courtyard pools. But it's not all the story of man's great tomorrows. Much of this $80 million show will be a glittering world of today. Dine atop the towering 60-story Space Needle which revolves to view Mt. Rainier, the Olympic and Cascade Ranges. Stroll Boulevards of the World filled with the sights and sounds of foreign lands. Thrill to the Monorail as it whisks you the mile from downtown Seattle in 95 seconds.

Rock 'n' Roll Is Here to Stay

Japanese-manufactured miniature transistors made pocket-size portable radios a necessity for sports and news addicts, as well as for any self-respecting teenager. Although the "Golden Age" of families gathered around a furniture-like receiver to catch serials was over, driving around listening to loud, tinny-sounding music had never been more popular.

Disc jockeys were the new pop-culture icons. Wolfman Jack ruled the Southwestern airwaves from a powerful Mexican transmitter, Cleveland/New York DJ Alan Freed—credited with coining the term *rock 'n' roll*—was one of the very first rock concert promoters. New York's Murray "the K" Kaufman followed Freed and produced fabled rock variety shows at Brooklyn's Fox and Paramount theaters.

Rock 'n' roll gave the powerful teenage consumer base a private language that simultaneously satisfied two primal urges: annoying parents and proving one's membership in a vast "secret" society.

Elizabeth Taylor Hilton Wilding Todd, widowed in 1958, fell for crooner Eddie Fisher. Unfortunately, Fisher was already married to Debbie Reynolds, America's Sweetheart. In 1959, Eddie promptly dumped Debbie to marry Liz. Taylor was soon on the set of *Cleopatra*, playing the Egyptian queen opposite Welsh actor Richard Burton as her lover Marc Antony. When the on-screen love story between Antony and Cleopatra turned into a real-life affair between Burton (also married) and Taylor, the movie became notorious before filming was even completed. When it finally wrapped at a cost of $44 million, *Cleopatra* became the most expensive movie ever made. With Liz paired up with Burton, Fisher was quickly history. The love triangle was criticized on the floor of Congress and even reached all the way to the Vatican, which condemned the illicit lovers. Burton and Taylor made it legal in '64 but were divorced ten years later. They would re-wed and divorce *again* in '76.

JFK Introduces the Peace Corps

President for a mere 39 days, JFK signed Executive Order 10924 on March 1, 1961, to create the Peace Corps. The undertaking was an effort to reach out to developing countries with an eye toward "peace and friendship." Volunteers with special skills in fields such as teaching, medicine, construction, and agriculture would share their abilities and pass them along to countries in Africa, South America, and Asia. The first group of Peace Corps volunteers numbered more than 5,000. They earned no salary while they ate, slept, and lived just like their hosts. The volunteers did, however, have the satisfaction of offering a decent way of life to a large segment of the world.

THE FIRST JAMES BOND FILM!

ARRY SALTZMAN and
ALBERT R. BROCCOLI PRESENT

IAN FLEMING'S

DR. NO

TECHNICOLOR

SEAN CONNERY AS 007

URSULA ANDRESS · JOSEPH WISEMAN · JACK LORD

DAWSON · MARSHALL KITZMILLER · GAYSON BERNARD LEE

Screenplay by RICHARD MAIBAUM JOHANNA HARWOOD BERKELY MATHER

Directed by TERENCE YOUNG

Produced by HARRY SALTZMAN ALBERT R. BROCCOLI EON PRODUCTIONS LTD.

British author Ian Fleming, partially inspired by spies he'd known during WWII, created one of the most successful fictional characters of all time in **James Bond,** aka 007

(the double-0 prefix bestowed "a license to kill"). Bond, first brought to the big screen by actor **Sean Connery** in *Dr. No,* was an ultrasophisticated womanizer with an extensive knowledge of almost everything, a preference for martinis "shaken, not stirred," and a wide assortment of futuristic gadgets. Millions of fans lusted after the secret agent's cynical cool, sleek Aston-Martin, and "Bond girls" with names such as Pussy Galore and Honey Ryder.

Motown Records made waves on the music charts. Led by Berry Gordy, Jr., a former Ford assembly-line worker, the self-proclaimed "sound of young America" introduced soul sensations such as the Supremes, Smokey Robinson and the Miracles, Marvin Gaye, Stevie Wonder, the Temptations, Mary Wells, Martha

Reeves, and the Four Tops. Key to Motown's early successes was the family atmosphere at the label: No star was too big to assist in the process. Singers answered phones while musicians slid vinyl into sleeves. Even crooner Marvin Gaye played drums behind other acts.

The Reverend Martin Luther King, Jr., Has a Dream

On August 28, 1963, nearly a quarter of a million citizens (a fifth of them white) converged on the Lincoln Memorial in the March on Washington for Jobs and Freedom. It was the largest such demonstration ever seen in the capital, and the first to be nationally televised. There was considerable star power present in the persons of Peter, Paul & Mary, Joan Baez, Bob Dylan (who performed "Only a Pawn in Their Game"), Ossie Davis, Odetta, Marian Anderson, Paul Newman, Lena Horne, Sidney Poitier, Marlon Brando, and more. But the day belonged to the Reverend Martin Luther King, Jr., who delivered one of America's most memorable orations in a stirring speech that became known as "I Have a Dream." After giving a short, factual talk, King was inspired to offer this astounding off-the-cuff narration when, as he was about to sit down, gospel singer Mahalia Jackson shouted out, "Tell them about your dream, Martin!" He did just that, electrifying a nation.

With its emphasis on a brave new future, the '60s spawned dozens of important technological and personal advances, many of which evolved into things Americans wouldn't be able to imagine living without.

Domino's (under the name DomiNick's in a single restaurant in Ypsilanti, Michigan) delivered its first pizza in 1960. That same year saw the invention of the ATM, the construction of the first hologram and the first laser, and an electronic larynx that gave speech to the previously mute.

Maybe it was because food could now be delivered to her door, but in 1961 Jean Nidetch, an overweight housewife from Queens, New York, developed a support system for herself and others who wished to drop pounds. She called it Weight Watchers.

The year after that, *Mutiny on the Bounty* became the first film to try the new wireless microphone. Silicon chips came on the market, as did silicone breast implants. The year 1962 also saw the invention of the first video computer game and the public introduction of touch-tone phones at the Seattle World's Fair. High-speed digital lines were installed in phone networks, and the Telstar communications satellite, which offered real-time television images around the globe, was launched. Sony began selling an open-reel home videotape recorder—forerunner of the VCR—in 1963, and Philips came out with the first audiocassette.

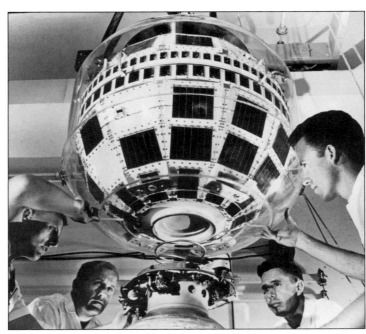

Ꮋonored at the Ɵscars

1960

Best Picture: *The Apartment* ▶

Best Actor: Burt Lancaster
(*Elmer Gantry*)

Best Actress: Elizabeth Taylor
(*Butterfield 8*)

1961

Best Picture: *West Side Story*

Best Actor: Maximilian Schell
(*Judgment at Nuremberg*)

Best Actress: Sophia Loren
◀ (*Two Women*)

1962

Best Picture: *Lawrence of Arabia* ▲

Best Actor: Gregory Peck (*To Kill a Mockingbird*)

Best Actress: Anne Bancroft (*The Miracle Worker*)

1963

Best Picture: *Tom Jones*

Best Actor: Sidney Poitier
◄ (*Lilies of the Field*)

Best Actress: Patricia Neal (*Hud*)

Fallen Hero

John Fitzgerald Kennedy
May 29, 1917–November 22, 1963

"Gentlemen . . . Excalibur has sunk
beneath the waves."

Texas Senator Ralph Yarborough to reporters outside
Parkland Hospital in Dallas, comparing JFK's demise
to the loss of the mythical sword of King Arthur.

Only a week after the murder of her husband, Jackie Kennedy shared her deepest thoughts with author Theodore White for *Life* magazine. She had already decided how she wanted the President and his administration to be remembered. Describing JFK's fondness for the 1960 Broadway musical *Camelot,* she characterized the President as "a man of magic," much like King Arthur. The nation, bereft over the assassination, jumped aboard the newly minted myth. Jackie quoted the title song from the musical—"Don't let it be forgot, that for one brief, shining moment, there was Camelot"—and set the context in which a United States in mourning would remember its President.

Chapter 2

Glad All Over

The **Dave Clark Five** took "Glad All Over" up to No. 6 in the charts in 1964. It was their first of eight Top Ten hits.

Beatlemania!!

The 1930s had Bing Crosby. The '40s had Frank Sinatra. In the '50s: Elvis. But the '60s belonged to four young Brits who brought jangling guitars, a driving beat, and shaggy hair to the shores of the United States. They were the Beatles, and they threw the country into a frenzy seldom seen before.

CBS News anchor Walter Cronkite compared Beatlemania to the D-Day invasion. Suddenly, every teenage boy wanted to trade in his crewcut for shaggy bangs, every teenage girl wanted a piece of the Beatles themselves, and everybody wanted a pair of pointed-toe "Beatle boots." In no time, America was snapping up Beatle pens, Beatle trading cards, Beatle wigs, Beatle dolls, Beatle board games, Beatle model kits—not to mention millions of Beatle record albums and 45s.

The influence of these four men from Liverpool, England, would soon reach far beyond music—into the worlds of fashion, film, and even religion and politics.

Let the High Jinks Ensue

As the decade progressed, TV comedy took a turn toward the goofy. There were still the family sitcoms we'd gotten used to, such as Dick Van Dyke as TV writer Rob Petrie, wed to the perkily sexy Laura, played by Mary Tyler Moore, in *The Dick Van Dyke Show;* or Fred MacMurray as Steve Douglas, dad to *My Three Sons.* But they shared prime time with the kooky,

spooky, ooky lives of *The Addams Family*—two-headed tortoises, bald-headed Uncle Festers, and all; *The Munsters*—another All-American family (with Frankenstein and Dracula as part of the family tree); Samantha Stevens, the beautiful witch-wife of husband Darrin, who cleaned the house

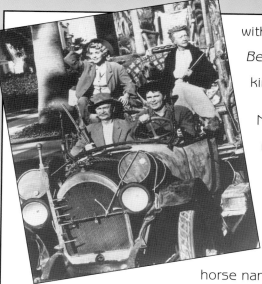

with a twitch of her cute little nose on *Bewitched;* and the transplanted bumpkins of *The Beverly Hillbillies*.

Not every popular situation comedy revolved around a family, however. *I Dream of Jeannie's* bottled-up genie lived with her astronaut "master" near Cape Kennedy, while a talking horse named *Mister Ed* refused to perform for anyone but his owner Wilbur. On *My Favorite Martian,* young Tim O'Hara helped an extraterrestrial survive a spaceship crash and kept him hidden by disguising him as his Uncle Martin. The clever POWs of *Hogan's Heroes* continually befuddled their silly Nazi captors as they ran a successful spy operation out of Stalag 13.

A New Heavyweight Champion

After winning Olympic gold, boxer **Cassius Marcellus Clay** turned pro. He was good, but no one expected him to defeat world heavyweight champ **Sonny Liston.** When their title bout started in February 1964, the younger and faster Clay had the overconfident Liston in trouble quickly.

After his victory, the new champion immediately announced that he had embraced the religion of the Black Muslims, a part of the Nation of Islam, and was forsaking his "slave name." He took the new name of Muhammad Ali.

The first frosh class of Baby Boomers started college in 1964. It's hardly surprising that all did not go smoothly. At **UC Berkeley,** the fall semester was not one of frat parties and panty raids. Constitutional rights were at stake, as students asserted their right to use campus property for civil rights activities. The **Free Speech Movement** was born, pitting protesting students against school administrators. Non-violent civil disobedience became common, as dissenting students were arrested for exercising their right to speak freely. Entertainers such as Joan Baez and Phil Ochs joined the cause, offering free concerts at student rallies.

By December, the conflict boiled over. More than a thousand students staged a "sit-in" in Sproul Hall, an administration building. Police arrested the trespassers with increasing viciousness, taking into custody nearly 800—the largest mass arrest in California history. The next day, more than 10,000 angry people gathered at the school plaza. By January 1965, the Free Speech Movement succeeded—amid the growing unrest on college campuses across America.

Host **Ed Sullivan** reliably offered a variety of performers each week on his show. They ranged from singers and comedians to acrobats and jugglers to the **puppet mouse Topo Gigio.** Although some believed they knew what was coming on the night of February 9, 1964, no one was really ready. The guests on that show included impressionist

Frank Gorshin and the Broadway cast of *Oliver!* However, most of America tuned in to see something else.

An estimated 70 million viewers watched the Beatles that evening. As teens in the audience shrieked and cried, John, Paul, George, and Ringo played five of their hits or soon-to-be hits. Sullivan would host the foursome twice more in February— providing a springboard to the total madness of Beatlemania.

EET HE BEATLES!

e First Album by England's Phenomenal Pop Combo

HIGH FIDELITY

The first American Beatles album took its task as an introduction to the group seriously. *Meet the Beatles* took the
second British Beatles album and replaced a few songs
with the gigantic single "I Want to Hold Your Hand" and its
B-side, then added "I Saw Her Standing There" from the
first British album for good measure. The cover of *Meet
the Beatles*, with the four mop-tops seriously, soberly
gazing at the viewer, became one of many iconic images
that defined the band.

The British Were Coming!
The British Were Coming!

When the Beatles took the country by storm, they opened the floodgates for other British rock groups to follow. In seeking a record contract, the Beatles had been turned down by nearly a dozen labels before EMI in England would take a chance—one that paid off big time. After that, no record label wanted to miss out on the **"next big British group,"** which resulted in opportunities for bands that might otherwise never have had them.

The Rolling Stones, fronted by the lithe and twitching Mick Jagger, quickly became known as the "bad boys" of rock 'n' roll. One appearance they

made on *The Ed Sullivan Show* in 1967 became an immediate scandal—the TV producers insisted they change the lyrics of their current hit from "Let's Spend the Night Together" to "Let's Spend Some Time Together."

British bands such as the Animals and the Kinks drew heavily from African-American R&B music. The Dave Clark 5 and other groups literally attempted to replicate the Beatles' success.

The impact of the British Invasion extended far beyond the music itself. For a time, Americans wanted long hair, Union Jack clothes—anything British.

The name Halston came to the forefront in '60s fashion. Born Roy Halston Frowick, the daring designer hit the decade running by designing the pillbox hat made famous by First Lady Jackie Kennedy. His name would soon become closely associated with high fashion.

But Halston wasn't the only fashion designer to make a bold statement. Austrian Rudi Gernreich shocked Americans in 1964 with the "monokini"—perhaps better known as the "top-less bathing suit." Those who dared to wear it were arrested for indecency, although modesty kept sales down to only the bravest of women.

The Magic Bus

Ken Kesey, the West Coast writer of such novels as *One Flew Over the Cuckoo's Nest,* became a counterculture icon after gathering a group of eclectic followers he called "the Merry Pranksters." Freely experimenting with the psychedelic drug LSD, they took an old bus and set out across the country in July 1964. Kesey filmed the trip, which was also described by Tom Wolfe in *The Electric Kool-Aid Acid Test.*

The Mustang

Sleek. Sporty. Built like a horse.

The Ford Mustang was **an American sports car** built in the tradition of the Ford Thunderbird and the Chevy Corvette. This revolutionary automobile with the long hood and the short trunk grabbed everyone's attention at the New York World's Fair in April 1964. Its sticker price of just over $2,000 was half the cost of the Corvette. But the brawny Mustang was a car that looked like no other. Built with a V-8 engine, the car **packed more than 270 horsepower** under the hood.

Peter Sellers

Already a successful comic actor in Britain as part of *The Goon Show*, Peter Sellers tickled America's funnybone in slapstick movies such as *The Pink Panther,* in which he played the **bumbling French Inspector Clouseau.** Stanley Kubrick's satire on atomic war, *Dr. Strangelove or: How I Learned to Stop Worrying and Love the Bomb,* found Sellers playing not one but three roles (earning one Oscar nomination). Sellers became the first male to grace the cover of *Playboy* magazine in April 1964—just one more distinction for a very rare performer.

Lyndon Baines Johnson was a professional politician. He had spent decades in Congress, eventually becoming Senate majority leader. Vice President to JFK, the tall Texan was thrust into the role of president after the 1963 assassination.

The following year found Johnson running for President himself, with the slogan "All the way with LBJ." He had picked up JFK's fallen torch for racial equality, pushing legislation for civil rights. He also championed a war on poverty for America's needy. Johnson was a master in domestic affairs.

Running against Johnson in 1964 was Arizona Senator Barry Goldwater. **"Au-H2O,"** the combined chemical symbols for gold and water, became synonymous with the Republican challenger. His far right-wing stance on domestic policies redefined the word *conservative*. Much of America recognized Goldwater as a fierce "hawk" who favored a strong American military stance in the escalating crisis in Vietnam.

The election that November resulted in one of the largest landslides in U.S. history. Goldwater was only able to win his home state and a handful of others in the Deep South. Johnson received strong support from the American public with more than 60 percent of the popular vote, clearing the way for what would become a tumultuous four years in office.

In Color
THE WORLD'S
FAIR OPENS

LIFE

MAY 1 · 1964 · 25¢

Built on the site of the 1939 World's Fair, the **New York World's Fair of 1964** offered a glimpse into the future. General Motors sponsored Futurama, where visitors could see dioramas of cities of tomorrow. Electronics giant IBM projected a nine-screen film on computer logic. The Bell System showed a history of communications with models and movies.

But attendance projections of 70 million visitors fell short by 20 million, and the World's Fair closed the next year, swimming in red ink.

The Rolling Stones song of that title was a tribute to tranquilizers such as Valium, which had become the No. 1 prescription drug in America by the mid-'60s. Users were running to the medicine cabinet to the tune of $250 million a year, and Valium became the drug of choice to treat the anxieties of everyday life.

Sensational Streisand

The young lady with the prominent nose and even more prominent singing voice hit the Broadway stage in 1962. By 1964, the 22-year-old Brooklyn-born Barbra Streisand landed the plum title role of the Broadway musical *Funny Girl.* Based on the life of vaudeville and radio star Fanny Brice, the show rocketed Streisand to fame.

Lenny Bruce on Trial

An edgy comic whose candid reflections on the world around him only seemed to get him into trouble, Lenny Bruce offered racy monologues with language that many found offensive. He had become a standup comedian in the 1950s, even appearing on Steve Allen's TV show in 1959. But as he pushed

the boundaries farther and farther, Bruce began to be arrested on obscenity charges across the U.S., from San Francisco to New York, from Los Angeles to Chicago. Convicted of obscenity, Bruce died in 1966 from a drug overdose.

Bob Dylan was the fresh voice of folk when, in June 1965, he took a left turn at the Newport Folk Festival. Instead of a traditional acoustic, Dylan strapped on an electric guitar and launched into "Maggie's Farm." The crowd's reaction is the subject of some dis-agreement. Legend has it that Dylan was booed for daring to grow, but some who were there insist other-wise. This story of the audi-ence's unhappiness spread, however, and the singer and his band were genuinely booed at later shows.

To the Moon!

Fashion designer Andre Courrèges claimed to be "the father of the miniskirt." However, his idea of the modern woman's wardrobe was best represented with his Moon Girl Collection. Worn across America, the collection featured white mini-dresses worn with white vinyl flat-soled "go-go" boots and other out-of-this-world accessories.

Although many in the toy industry assumed boys would never play with dolls, **Hasbro** figured otherwise and created four distinct military combat characters, one for each branch of the armed services. Eventually, however, they committed to just one: GI Joe.

Joe was an 11½-inch "action figure" (never call it a "doll") articulated like an artist's wooden figure model. A full complement of uniforms, weapons, and vehicles made GI Joe "the complete fighting man."

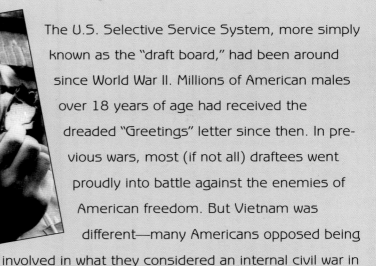

The U.S. Selective Service System, more simply known as the "draft board," had been around since World War II. Millions of American males over 18 years of age had received the dreaded "Greetings" letter since then. In previous wars, most (if not all) draftees went proudly into battle against the enemies of American freedom. But Vietnam was different—many Americans opposed being involved in what they considered an internal civil war in Asia. A substantial number of those Americans chose to protest the war and the draft by publicly burning their Selective Service registrations, or draft cards. President Johnson signed a law in 1965 that made the burning of these cards a criminal offense, but that action merely served to incite more burnings at antiwar demonstrations.

In 1966, a young man named David Paul O'Brien burned his draft card in Boston. He was arrested, tried, and convicted of the crime; his appeal eventually reached the U.S. Supreme Court in 1968. The court, headed by Chief Justice Earl Warren, upheld the law and the conviction.

Pop Goes the Art!

Exit Dada, enter Pop Art: For a radically different postwar era, a shockingly new artform was required. This post-modern movement, launched in England in the late 1950s, now burst upon American public consciousness via illustrator Andy Warhol's ironic portraits of Campbell's Soup cans and Brillo boxes. Warhol's name, image, and work became even more recognizable than that of Picasso. Many people believe his quip that in the future, everyone would be famous for 15 minutes may have been correct.

Pop Art often commented upon America's insatiable consumerism and the emptiness it strove to conceal. British emigre David Hockney painted a series of canvases depicting the swimming pools in his new hometown of Los Angeles. The first superheroes painted by Mel Ramos evolved into

nude girlie pin-ups juxtaposed with brand products. Jasper Johns was inspired by coat hangers, flags, and other everyday objects. Robert Indiana, best known for his iconic "Love" paintings, found his muse in traffic signs. Roy Lichtenstein appropriated bold outlines and word balloons from art in romance and war comic books, while George Segal wrapped models in medical bandages to create the life-size plaster casts that spoke to modern alienation and loneliness. Many scratched their heads at the meaning of it all, but younger audiences immediately "got it." Gallery retrospectives continue to demonstrate these artists' ability to forecast what was left of the 20th century.

At the Fillmore

Wolfgang Grajonca fled the Holocaust, changed his name to **Bill Graham,** and settled in the Bay Area in the mid–1950s. In his position as manager of the San Francisco Mime Troupe, Graham **arranged two rock benefits at a crumbling old auditorium called the Fillmore** in 1965 and decided that booking shows was his new vocation. Relocating to the Carousel, he renamed it the Fillmore—which became the Fillmore West when a sister venue opened in New York City. The Avalon, Graham's main San Francisco competition, soon capitulated, essentially leaving the city's

entire music scene in his hands. Similar monopolies have been disastrous, but Graham became the gold standard for all rock promoters by providing top value for concertgoers (seated venues with quality sound, sightlines, light shows, and security; mind-expanding combinations of acts) and catering to musicians—when he wasn't threatening or shouting at them.

When **posters** and **handbills** promoting shows at the Fillmore first went up in a **burst of color and energy equal to the music itself,** they also announced the flowering of the Bay Area's underground counterculture. At that time, there were no radio spots or newspaper ads to announce concerts—instead, word was spread on the street by the works of artists such as Stanley Mouse, **Rick Griffin,** Victor Moscoso, Alton Kelley, Wes Wilson, Bonnie MacLean, and David Singer. Their inspirations ranged from 19th-century Art Nouveau to 20th-century psychedelics in creating the vivid visuals that subsequently moved from brick walls into museum collections.

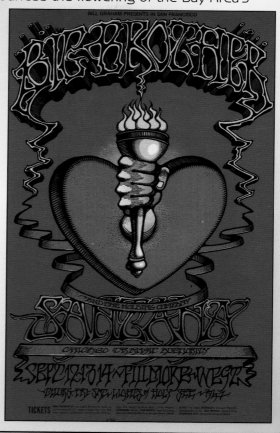

Art Arfons's *Green Monster* and Craig Breedlove's *Spirit of America* revolutionized speed racing with hand-built vehicles equipped with jet engines. They were similar to Art's brother Walt Arfons's *Wingfoot Express,* shown here with driver Bobby Tatroe. Art Arfons shattered land speed records in May 1964 by reaching 434 mph on the salt flats of Bonneville, Utah. Tatroe challenged that record in September 1965 but couldn't meet it. Craig Breedlove met it, however, and then some, clocking over 555 in November 1965. A week later, while trying to retake the title, Arfons miraculously survived a crackup at 576 mph. Breedlove then broke 600 mph—a speed Arfons was never able to beat.

The 8-track tape cartridge took off in 1966 when Ford began offering players as optional equipment on its new automobiles. Over 60,000 were installed that first year, making 8-track the first prerecorded tape format to reach a national mass market.

The Spy Craze

Maybe it was JFK's fondness for the fictional James Bond, or perhaps it was the heightened tension of the Cold War, but a sudden craze for spies took hold in the middle of the

decade. British TV offered **The Avengers,** which teamed a proper Englishman with a cooly sexy sidekick (Diana Rigg's catsuits inspired many an adolescent coming-of-age). American TV responded with **The Man from U.N.C.L.E.,** in which the Bondesque Napoleon Solo was assisted by Russian Illya Kuryakin; *The Wild, Wild West,* which featured a highly equipped Secret Service agent working for President Ulysses Grant on the Western frontier (!), and *I Spy,* featuring two agents undercover as a tennis star and his trainer. *I Spy* was the first TV drama to cast an African-American (Bill Cosby) in a starring role. Spoofs such as **Get Smart** and *Our Man Flint* could also be found, as could plenty of merchandising: spy pens, realistic replica guns, board games, fan clubs, scale models of James Bond's cars, figurines, and much more.

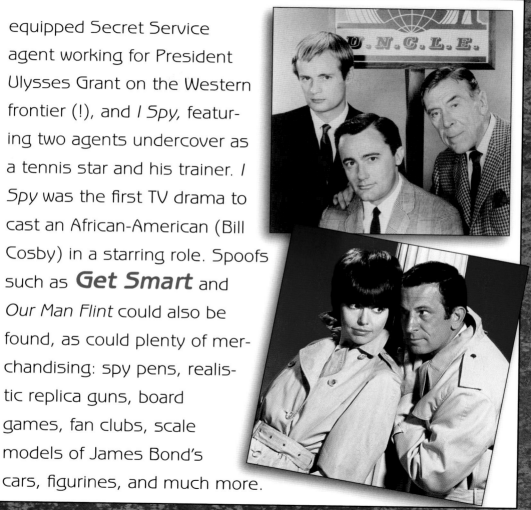

While there's some argument about who actually invented the miniskirt, **British designer Mary Quant popularized the leggy style,** to the delight of males everywhere. By 1966, the mini had already become one of the decade's defining style statements. The look was advanced by the invention of opaque pantyhose, which preserved a modicum of modesty, and balanced by short boots or low-heeled Mary Jane-strapped shoes. England also gave the world the original "waif" model in ultra-skinny teenage Twiggy, who

was emulated by young girls down to her painted-on lower lashes; Mattel even produced a doll in her image. Meanwhile, male peacockery was being indulged by the trendy boutiques lining London's newly fashionable Carnaby Street, which helped promote brightly colored shirts, wildly patterned wide ties, and Edwardian-style suits for the stylish young man. Beatle boots and shaggy hairstyles were optional—but encouraged. The **mod** look was here.

Life in a Small Town

Peyton Place was the story of a small town drenched in darkness and scandalous romance. As a best-selling novel by Grace Metalious and an Oscar-nominated film in the 1950s, it raised more than a few eyebrows across the country.

When the ABC television network introduced *Peyton Place* as a weekly series in September 1964, it was the first soap opera to find itself in prime time. The steamy side of the New England town had to be toned down a bit for the small screen, but it still made for great water-cooler conversations. *Peyton Place* also launched the acting careers of performers Mia Farrow and Ryan O'Neal.

The End of the Baby Boom

The years after World War II saw what came to be called the Baby Boom, which produced some 78 million children from 1946 to 1964. This unprecedented population growth slowly leveled off until birthrates reached a new low of 17.5 per 1,000 in 1968 (compared to 27 per 1,000 in 1947). By 1971, the idea of a "birth dearth" was being floated because expectations of Boomer females creating an "echo boom" were unfulfilled—these young women were having fewer children than their mothers. Various reasons were suggested for this, but whatever the cause, it appeared that the seemingly endless expansion and optimism of the 1950s was now truly over.

The Supremes

In late 1964, a chemist named Norman Stingley concocted a compound made from synthetic rubber. Molded under thousands of pounds of pressure, the sphere had a lot of bounce to the ounce.

The Wham-O Company took Stingley's idea and created a dark rubber "Super Ball" of just less than two inches in diameter, made from a space-age material called Zectron. But this was no ordinary orb—the high resiliency rate meant that once the ball bounced, it continued to bounce . . . and bounce . . . and bounce. Many children engaged in contests, seeing who could bounce their Super Ball the highest or how many bounces they could get from a single throw. Hours of fun could be had in just trying to catch it.

When the **Houston Astrodome** opened in April 1965, some called it the Eighth Wonder of the World. The first domed sports stadium was a marvel of architectural engineering, and it revolutionized the sports experience by excluding inclement weather and introducing artificial grass (named AstroTurf after the stadium itself), giant scoreboards, cushioned seats, and VIP skyboxes.

Blackout!

The lights—and everything else dependent upon electricity—went out in New York City shortly before 5:30 P.M. on November 9, 1965. Without TV to watch or much else to do, New Yorkers supposedly got busy instead: *The New York Times* featured articles the following August alleging a spike in births nine months later. In fact, a statistical analysis showed that there had been no "blackout baby boom"—but this most congenial of urban myths still persists.

Cutting-Edge Computing

Computer manufacturer IBM bet the farm with a bold move in 1964 when it scrapped several successful lines **to finance System/360**—a series of five increasingly powerful business computers that, for the first time, were compatible with each other. Until this time, each computer was unique to each customer, and for every upgrade, software applications had to be rewritten and peripherals extensively modified. By 1970, hundreds of products that worked with System/360 models had been introduced by IBM's competitors.

Inspired by Bob Dylan's folk rock, **the Byrds** formed in Los Angeles in 1964. The group covered several Dylan songs on its debut album, which was characterized by soaring harmonies and "chiming" Rickenbacker guitars. Like many groups, the Byrds experienced shifting lineups. Shown here in 1967 are Chris Hillman, David Crosby, Michael Clarke, and Roger (formerly Jim) McGuinn. Gene Clark, songwriter and vocalist, had left a year earlier, his fear of flying interfering with an extensive touring schedule.

Danger, Will Robinson!

Baby Boomers were charmed by *Lost in Space* when the Robinson family, along with their trusty robot and the dastardly Dr. Smith, blasted off for Alpha Centauri in September 1965 (the show was optimistically set in 1997).

Although the series made the Top 10 by its sixth episode, its popularity bewildered CBS brass. But it had an obvious appeal to kids: Children were presented as heroes, and the fantasy was fun. Producer Irwin Allen was also responsible for the TV series *Voyage to the Bottom of the Sea, The Time Tunnel,* and *Land of the Giants.*

The seven castaways
of *Gilligan's Island,* shipwrecked during
a three-hour tour, somehow had endless
resources and a genius inventor who could build anything
out of a couple of coconuts. But no one in their merry band
seemed to have the skills necessary to patch a hole in a boat.

Life's a Beach

Frankie Avalon and former Mouseketeer **Annette Funicello** starred in a series of beach and bikini movies with clever names such as *Beach Party, Muscle Beach Party, Bikini Beach,* and ***Beach Blanket Bingo.*** The beach was essentially an expansive backyard, where everyone was on perpetual summer vacation, adults were silly (if present at all), and work, like any other disturbing reality, was nonexistent. It was the Garden of Eden—with sand.

Radical youth group Students for a Democratic Society (SDS) was organized in Ann Arbor, Michigan, in 1960. Initially focusing on inner-city woes, by the middle of the decade SDS was the most vocal faction of young people opposed to the military draft and the Vietnam War. The first "teach-in," held on March 24, 1965, at the University of Michigan, attracted 3,000 students and faculty to workshops, debates, and lectures. Soon, similar events were being conducted at dozens of other campuses around the country, such as this one at the University of California. By October 1966, SDS membership was estimated at 25,000.

Board games for all ages grew in popularity. Milton Bradley was a name known to kids everywhere. **The Game of Life,** which used a spinner rather than dice to determine how many spaces to move, and **Stratego** came on the market for the first time.

Other popular board games that debuted in the '60s included Mousetrap, Operation, Mystery Date, and Battleship.

The Beatles continued to astonish, morphing from lovable moptops into psychedelic seers. The cover of their ninth album from Capital Records, 1965's *Rubber Soul,* with its

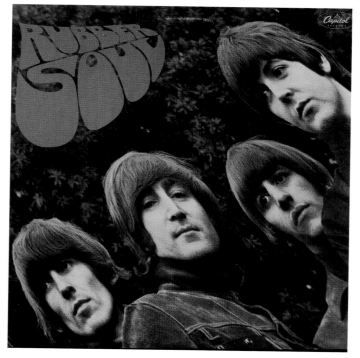

distorted fish-eye view of the group, was the first sign that something weird was going on. The disc inside stunned fans with **one of rock's first multicultural forays** via George Harrison's sitar. It also featured increasingly personal compositions from John Lennon and a careful construction in which songs flowed into, or subtly commented upon, each other.

THE GROOVY SIDE OF THE '60s 🌼 107

Chapter 3

Good Vibrations

In 1966, the Beach Boys achieved their third No. 1 hit when "Good Vibrations" topped the charts.

Nobody likes a war, but the United States always had the backing of its people . . . until Vietnam. To many, the conflict in the small Southeast Asian country was none of America's business. Those who opposed the war and the effort to draft U.S. soldiers sought relief through various means. The phrases *conscientious objector* and *draft dodger* became familiar across the country, while somewhere between 20,000 and 90,000 protested the draft by escaping to the immunity of Canada.

Still others sought the cynical recommendations of a book published in 1966 called *1001 Ways to Beat the Draft* by Tuli Kupferberg and Robert Bashlow. Kupferberg, the lead singer for an eclectic band named the Fugs, suggested off-beat tactics such as "marry your sister," "ask what's in it for you," "become the publisher of the Little Mao Tse-Tung Library," and "grope J. Edgar Hoover."

No record was ever kept of how many draft dodgers followed Kupferberg's advice or how effective it may have been.

It was a mere mile-and-a-half section of street in Los Angeles. For years it had featured supper clubs—Ciro's, the Tracadero, and the Mocambo—frequented by movie legends, and it had been immortalized by stylish detectives on TV's *77 Sunset Strip*. But that had all changed by 1966,

when the Sunset Strip had become a hangout for rockers and teenyboppers. Local police began to see the Strip as nothing more than a rowdy stretch of road, and when they began enforcing a 10 P.M. curfew for kids under 18, more than 1,000 people went on a rampage.

The Mamas and the Papas—John Phillips, wife Michelle, Cass Elliot, and Denny Doherty—were another big group on the folk/rock scene. Their hits, such as "California Dreamin'," "Monday, Monday," "Words of Love," and "Dedicated to the One I Love," blended the quartet's voices in harmony.

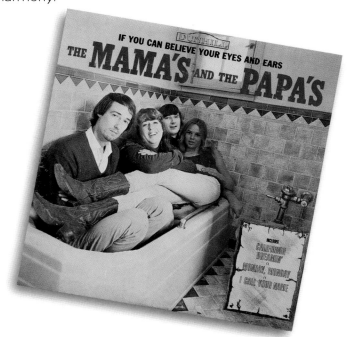

Acid Tests

It went by various names: LSD, acid. But this powerful, mind-altering hallucino-genic drug was officially listed as lysergic acid diethylamide. Harvard psychology professor Timothy Leary found its brain-bending effects fascinating and began his own experiments, or "acid tests." Believing its use could open up new worlds for those who sought "alternative answers to life," Leary formed the "League of Spiritual Discovery" and began to promote the recreational use of LSD to the public.

The U.S. Food and Drug Administration moved quickly in 1966 to outlaw the manufacture and use of LSD, but that did little to deter the ongoing search for "the perfect trip."

Cult film director Russ Meyer may have been the father of the "sexploitation" film, which was generally loaded with large-breasted women and gratuitous violence. The low-budget, black-and-white **Faster, Pussycat! Kill! Kill!** is a crown jewel of the genre, featuring strippers turned murderers, with drag-racing and kidnapping thrown in for good measure.

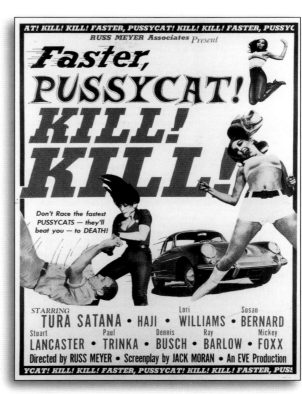

Perhaps tame by 21st-century standards, Meyer's work shocked moviegoers of the time.

Let's Go Disco

With a name literally meaning "record library," discotheques were dance clubs that played recorded music rather than featuring live bands. Originally started in France during World War II, discotheques became the home of **"go-go" dancers** and **record-spinning DJs** in 1960s America. The Whiskey A-Go-Go in Los Angeles and the Peppermint Lounge in New York City were two prominent discotheques.

Who's Afraid of Taylor and Burton?

After Elizabeth Taylor and Richard Burton starred in *Who's Afraid of Virginia Woolf?* in 1966, previous screen husband-and-wife teams such as Rock Hudson and Doris Day were left behind in the dust. Based on the Edward Albee play, the film intro- duced Ameri- can audiences to foul lan-

guage and bickering never before seen between enemies on the silver screen, let alone married couples.

A wife, a mother, and a working woman, Betty Friedan became a major voice for women's rights after writing *The Feminine Mystique* in 1963. The best-selling book focused on women's roles as housekeeper and child-bearer and the search for feminine identity in America.

In 1966, Friedan became the first president of a new activist group called NOW,

the National Organization for Women. The group committed itself to establishing educational, employment, and business opportunities for women and securing an equal place for them in American society.

The Double Darrens

As Samantha Stevens in *Bewitched,* Elizabeth Montgomery starred with two different actors playing her husband, Darren. Which Darren was your favorite?

Dick York *(opposite)*
Dick Sargent *(left)*

Robert McNamara, former president of Ford Motors and a Harvard graduate, became Secretary of Defense under JFK and remained in that position under LBJ. McNamara returned to his alma mater on November 7, 1966, to make a speech and was confronted by angry Vietnam War protesters. When he tried to address them, they shouted him down, and he had to be rescued by the police. President Johnson would announce McNamara's resignation later that same month, when the secretary stepped down to head the World Bank.

"I spent four of the happiest years on the Berkeley campus doing some of the same things you're doing here. But there was one important difference: I was both tougher and more courteous."

Robert McNamara,
addressing hostile Harvard students

Brit Folk

The hot Scot named Donovan was Britain's answer to American folkie Bob Dylan. Known only by his first name, the folk-rock singer with the curly hair found success on U.S. radio with hits such as "Jennifer Juniper," "Hurdy Gurdy Man," "Wear Your Love Like Heaven," "Sunshine Superman," and "Mellow Yellow."

Simon and Garfunkel

Tom and Jerry were famous as cat and mouse cartoon characters, but the names were also used by a folk singing duo in the late '50s. Their first single, "Hey Schoolgirl," barely broke the charts.

Fast forward to the mid–'60s, when that same musical duo was known as Simon and Garfunkel. Their smooth blend of folk and rock music produced Top 40 hits such as "The Sounds of Silence," "Homeward Bound," "I Am a Rock," and "Mrs. Robinson."

Pontiac introduced the first muscle car in the GTO, a mid-size with a large engine for extra power. With an acceleration from 0 to 60 in 6.5 seconds, the model grew to huge popularity. The GTO sold almost 100,000 models in 1966.

The world of fashion was reborn with the introduction of the "supermodel." Stunningly gorgeous, these fashion icons graced the covers of magazines such as *Glamour*, *Vogue*, and *Harper's Bazaar*. The new top trio in fashion were waif-thin Twiggy, statuesque Veruschka, and exotic **Jean Shrimpton.**

Stylishly wearing the latest "mod" designs, they had their lovely tresses styled by innovators such as Vidal Sassoon, and their images were captured on film by Richard Avedon, David Bailey, and other creative photographers.

These lovely ladies were "in"... as in, "incredible."

Masters and Johnson

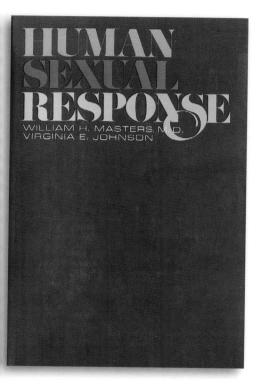

Pioneers in researching what made America tick between the bedsheets, Doctors William Masters and Virginia Johnson saw the published findings of their 12-year study, *Human Sexual Response*, top the best-seller lists. The popular book revealed America's desire to loosen its reserved outlook on sex and physical relationships.

More Popular Than Whom?

Everyone says something they wish they hadn't—even a world-famous Beatle.

John Lennon was quoted in a London newspaper as saying, "Christianity will go. We're more popular than Jesus now. I don't know which will go first—rock and roll or Christianity." Many Americans took the comment out of context, and the result was vicious. Organized protest groups, some spurred on by dissenting radio stations, collected once-revered Beatle albums for burning in bonfires. It was an ugly scene.

Lennon later apologized, offering that his comments referred to the unstable state of religion rather than the popularity of his band. "I suppose if I'd said television was more popular than Jesus, I would've gotten away with it."

Jacqueline Susann, a sometime-actress turned author, rewrote the romance field of books with *Valley of the Dolls.* The novel, telling the story of three women anxious to make it big in their careers and falling to the perils of drugs and sex, became 1966's top-selling book.

Blow-Up shocked America with its fleeting glimpses of female nudity. Directed by Michelangelo Antonioni and starring David Hemmings and Vanessa Redgrave, this British film told the story of a bohemian London fashion photographer who may have unintentionally captured a murder on film.

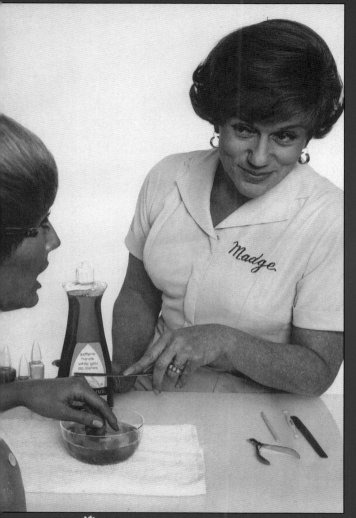

You're Soaking in It

Manicurists across America took the hint when Madge, **Palmolive Dishwashing Liquid's** TV spokesperson, started using the pretty green stuff to soften hands in commercials. Actress Jan Minor shocked beauty salon customers when she revealed their hands were "soaking in it." A later survey showed that many parlors in America actually used Palmolive to soften customer's hands.

The use of high-powered microwave radiation to cook food began in the 1940s with enormous microwave ovens—almost six feet tall and weighing 750 pounds. Amana changed all that with its Radarange, the first compact countertop microwave oven. Competitors soon leaped into the market.

Strike!

American-born migrant worker Cesar Chavez never went further in school than the eighth grade, but he continued to educate himself. His study of Gandhi and St. Francis influenced his leadership of *La Causa* in the fight for social justice. In 1962, Chavez founded what became the United Farm Workers union. Three years later, he emerged as a focal figure for striking grape pickers seeking a raise in wages to $1.40 an hour. Chavez's call to boycott California table grapes eventually spread to Canada and Europe, and the longest labor strike in U.S. history ended in 1970 with the grape pickers' nonviolent victory.

Hey, Hey, They're the Monkees!

Davy Jones

Mike Nesmith

Peter Tork

Mickey Dolenz

"I'm a Believer"

"Last Train to Clarksville"

"(I'm Not Your) Steppin' Stone"

"Pleasant Valley Sunday"

"Daydream Believer"

The Endless Summer

On any day of the year it's summer somewhere in the world. Bruce Brown's latest color film highlights the adventures of two young American surfers, Robert August and Mike Hynson who follow this everlasting summer around the world. Their unique expedition takes them to Senegal, Ghana, Nigeria, South Africa, Australia, New Zealand, Tahiti, Hawaii and California. Share their experiences as they search the world for that perfect wave which may be forming just over the next Horizon. **BRUCE BROWN FILMS**

Bruce Brown Films the producer of "Slippery When Wet," "Surf Crazy," "Barefoot Adventure," "Surfing Hollow Days," "Waterlogged" and "The Endless Summer."

Documentaries seldom drew much attention in the '60s, but *The Endless Summer* was different. Director Bruce Brown took filmgoers to exotic lands such as Hawaii, Australia, Ghana, and Tahiti, where he offered a **breathtaking view of the popular surfing scene,** as two young men traveled the world in search of the perfect wave.

Pop music got a shot of East Indian influence when some rock stars, the Rolling Stones' Brian Jones and the Beatles' George Harrison, for example, began incorporating the stinging whine of the 19-stringed sitar into their songs. Never before heard in Western music, sitar virtuoso Ravi Shankar became an overnight star in his own right.

*A **Fistful of Dollars*** was the first of a film genre known as the **"spaghetti western"** to strike international success. Made in Italy in 1964, it took almost three years to reach American shores. When the movie finally had its U.S. premiere, the rugged face and silent squint of TV actor Clint Eastwood proved the performer was a budding superstar as "The Man with No Name."

Another movie actor who'd gained success in Westerns as host of TV's *Death Valley Days*, **Ronald Reagan** received his first taste of politics when he was elected president of the Screen Actors Guild in 1947. It must have agreed with him. Nearly 20 years later, the star of *Knute Rockne All American* and *Bedtime for Bonzo* would continue his political climb when California constituents voted to "win one for the Gipper" by electing him governor.

Television producer Chuck Barris struck gold when *The Dating Game* hit the airwaves on ABC in 1965. Three anxious bachelors or bachelorettes were anonymously interviewed by a comely young lady or virile young man who then would choose one of them for a "dream date." Hosted by smooth-voiced Jim Lange, each episode would end with everyone throwing a big kiss to the cameras.

Your Mission, Should You Choose to Accept It...

In *Mission: Impossible*, TV viewers were offered an exciting world of spies, high-tech gadgets, disguises, mystery, and espionage. Jim Phelps of the Impossible Missions Force received assignments from an anonymous prerecorded voice—always before the tape self-destructed in five seconds.

While having the world's greatest crooner for a father didn't hurt, **Nancy Sinatra** made her own name in music. Her No. 1 single, "These Boots Are Made for Walkin'," hit the top of the charts in February 1966. A year later, she struck gold again (in a duet with dad) with "Somethin' Stupid."

The lady with the great backhand started playing tennis at age 11 and had first won Wimbledon in 1962 at age 18. In 1967, Billie Jean King won every U.S. and British singles, doubles, and mixed doubles tournament—the first woman to do that in a single year since Alice Marble in 1938.

Along with the Filmore Auditorium and Winterland, the **Avalon Ballroom** was the center of San Francisco's rock music scene. Up-and-coming bands such as Jefferson Airplane, the Grateful Dead, Janis Joplin with Big Brother and the Holding Company, the Doors, Quicksilver Messenger Service, and the Youngbloods graced the stage at Sutter and Van Ness streets. Steppenwolf; Creedence Clearwater Revival; Blood, Sweat & Tears; and others got their first major exposure at the Avalon before it closed in bankruptcy in 1968.

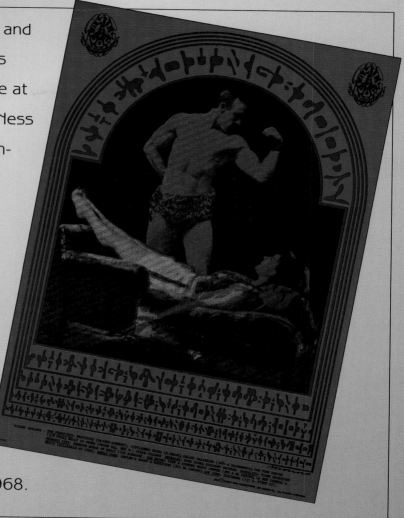

Holy TV Craze!

In a new look at an old super-hero, a campy, tongue-in-cheek version of *Batman* came to the airwaves. With Adam West and Burt Ward in the lead roles of Batman and Robin, the twice-a-week show quickly shot to the top of the ratings and kicked off its own brand of Batmania. Seeking to attract adult viewers as well as kids, *Batman* lined up big-name guest stars such as Burgess Meredith, Vincent Price, Milton Berle, and Liberace as villains.

The ABC network pursued its bat theme in daytime programming, as well. Television soap operas were populated with broken romances, illicit affairs, and ambitious young bucks until producer Dan Curtis introduced **Dark Shadows.** Central character Barnabas Collins, played by Jonathan Frid, was a vampire who haunted the Collinwood mansion, where he encountered ghosts, werewolves, and other assorted members of the netherworld.

Although the surfin' sounds of **the Beach Boys** dominated radio in the early '60s, the British Invasion had come to overshadow the band. Led by Brian Wilson, the group performed music that told of teenage crushes, cruising in a T-Bird, and searching for the perfect wave. Influenced by the Beatles' *Rubber Soul,* however, Wilson began to make music unlike anything he'd written before in songs such as "Wouldn't It Be Nice" and "Good Vibrations" and in the widely acclaimed album

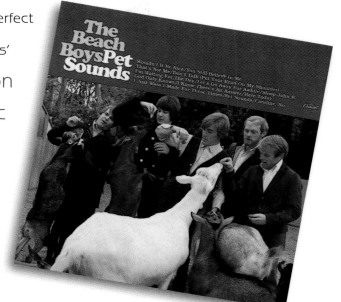

Pet Sounds. The cross-pollination continued when Paul McCartney credited *that* album as a main influence for the Beatles' *Sgt. Pepper's Lonely Hearts Club Band.* Paul continued to identify *Pet Sounds* as his favorite album into the 21st century.

Live Long and Prosper

It was a TV show in which the ratings were low and one of the main characters had green blood—hardly the stuff of which successful programs are made. Creator and producer Gene Roddenberry premiered *Star Trek* on NBC. But when the network announced the cancellation of the series after two seasons of mediocre ratings, it was deluged by an enormous barrage of fan letters. This salvaged the series for one more year—to go where no show had gone before.

Chapter 4

All You Need Is Love

The Beatles debuted "All You Need Is Love" on *One World*, the first live global satellite broadcast, on June 25, 1967. The international audience for the show is estimated to have been in the hundreds of millions.

The Summer of Love

Much of the 1960s counterculture centered around a neighbor-hood in San Francisco called Haight-Ashbury. It was there that **"hippies" first arrived on the scene**—long-haired, unshaven, seeking only peace, love, and a constant high.

The summer of 1967 became known as the Summer of Love and attracted thousands of hippies to the Haight-Ashbury district, which soon became a mecca for alternative businesses and lifestyles. The citizens of the Haight simply wanted to save America from the Vietnam War, from a government that couldn't be trusted, and from a world that seemed to be in constant conflict.

But the district drew more than just peace-seeking, drug-imbibing love children. Estimates of more than 100,000 hippies were balanced with more than 100,000 tourists who flocked to see how the other half lived. Gray Line added the Haight to its bus tour of San Francisco in 1967.

The Grateful Dead

The granddaddy of psychedelic jam bands came into being in San Francisco in 1965 as the Warlocks, but they renamed themselves with a phrase from an Egyptian prayer discovered by one-time banjo aficionado Jerry Garcia, who now played guitar. The genial Garcia **earned the fond nickname Captain Trips** after the Dead's house-band stint at author Ken Kesey's legendary LSD parties, the Acid Tests. Adding to the drug-induced delight, chemist Owsley Stanley provided funds for the group's communal Haight-Ashbury house. Many free concerts later, the Grateful Dead was a top area draw, but it wasn't until 1970 that the group broke through nationally with FM hits such as "Uncle John's Band" and "Truckin'."

Hippie Chicks

Young followers of the new, free-spirited ethos went by a variety of names. "Flower children" was one popular appellation. "Hippie chicks" described young girls who eschewed makeup and hairstyling for the natural look, which echoed their back-to-the-earth ideas and choice of apparel—often embroidered cotton peasant blouses or similar ethnic garb, accessorized with flowing skirts or patched jeans. They never wore brassieres or foundation garments. Such creatures were thought to be proponents of "free love" (i.e., casual sex) and were often found selling homemade goods or dervish-dancing at Grateful Dead concerts.

Advertising that doubled as fine art was not a new idea—it began in the 19th century with Toulouse-Lautrec—but it was '60s **San Francisco artist Joe McHugh who developed a hippie cottage industry with ad posters.** The surreal *Alice in Wonderland*, also a work of the previous century, inspired McHugh's 1967 piece "White Rabbit" (created independently of the similarly named Jefferson Airplane hit song). This iconic image eventually sold hundreds of thousands of copies through newly created venues—poster and head shops.

The week of October 16, 1967, became another memorable period in the growing unrest over the Vietnam War. **Stop the Draft Week** was announced to create a **nationwide campaign for peace marches** and to disrupt the military's draft induction centers.

In Oakland, things grew ugly as more than 4,000 protesters filled the streets, forcing police to call in reinforcements from San Francisco. "Peace" demonstrators were seen overturning cars, as well as throwing bottles, tin cans, and rocks.

As a climax to the week, yippies, hippies, professors, radicals, ministers, mothers, and Maoists, along with novelist Norman Mailer and pediatrician Dr. Benjamin Spock, gathered at the Lincoln Memorial. They had come in car pools, buses, trains, and from as far afield as California. Police were armed with tear gas to contain a crowd of more than 50,000 as it ranted at the Pentagon, the military-industrial complex made manifest.

On Capitol Hill, the House of Representatives was locked down for fear of invasion. Abbie Hoffman asked for a permit to "levitate" the Pentagon building and thereby "exorcise" it of evil (it stayed put). By the end of that chaotic day, there had been 200 arrests and 13 reported injuries.

Actor/producer Warren Beatty was onto something when he nagged Warner Brothers into releasing **Bonnie and Clyde.** The movie's nihilistic violence, sympathetic treatment of '30s-era outlaw lovers, and disregard for previous convention riled critics but drew young viewers in droves. Costar

Faye Dunaway's slouchy outfits even sparked a revival of period fashion. Hailed by *Time* magazine as heralding the advent of "New Cinema," the film eventually grossed millions and received 10 Oscar nominations.

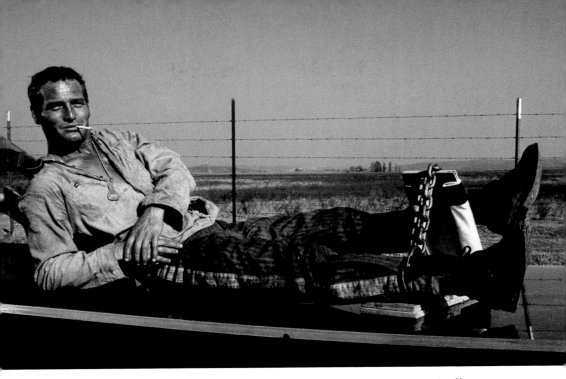

"What we have here is a failure to communicate" became a catchphrase after Strother Martin's laconic line delivery in **Cool Hand Luke,** which starred Paul Newman as the eponymous hunky convict. The film's youthful audience appreciated the character's antihero rebelliousness while confined to a Southern chain gang for a minor offense. In his refusal to submit to authority, remaining defiant in the face of overwhelming power, Luke embodied the protest movements of the era.

Right Hand, Green!

Physical board games were catching on in America. One inventor fashioned footpads of various colors that kids would wear, matching the colors on a large polka-dotted floor grid. He called it Pretzel. Milton Bradley picked up the game and called it Twister. After Johnny Carson popularized it on *The Tonight Show*, it sold more than 3 million units in its very first year.

Roughly five years after **Elvis Presley** moved his underage love into Graceland, the King finally made it legal in Las Vegas on May 1, 1967, with former Army brat Priscilla Beaulieu. She gave birth to their daughter, Lisa Marie, exactly nine months to the day after the wedding.

The Human Be-In

The first Human Be-In, held in San Francisco's Golden Gate Park on January 14, 1967, was a free festival that attracted around 20,000 and brought together two previously unaffiliated factions: the city's hippie population and the politically active counterculture. Celebrants were encouraged to **wear whatever expressed their "inner selves," from tie-dye to saris.** Ignoring stage events that included the likes

of Allen Ginsberg and the Grateful Dead, celebrants peacefully wandered, played music, and shared marijuana joints.

Flower Power

Poet Allen Ginsberg has been credited with coining the term "flower power," a phrase that encapsulated a belief system that entailed showing love and living in harmony. It rejected modern society's rules involving war, materialism, and the destruction of the earth's natural gifts.

Adherents of flower power experimented with altered states of awareness and sometimes entered into communal, mutually supportive living conditions, which often included the sharing of partners and raising of children. They preferred spiritualism to organized religion, taking cues from America's original indigenous inhabitants and other ancient peaceful peoples.

Flower-power followers tried to sustain human existence without creating needless waste or harming animals, embracing ways of valuing other people minus the trappings of artificial status or preconceived ideals of beauty.

From 1966 to 1970, the four years **Jimi Hendrix reigned supreme,** he astonished audiences and demolished other guitarists with his audacious exploration of the instrument's outer-limits possibilities. Chas Chandler, bassist for the Animals, "discovered" Hendrix in Greenwich Village and brought him back to London to create the Jimi Hendrix Experience. Hendrix's breakthrough Monterey Pop performance led to the headlining spot at Woodstock, where his anguished, wordless version of "The Star-Spangled Banner" forever changed the national anthem. Hendrix's guitar pyrotechnics and songwriting skills were matched only by his flamboyant personal style—as Grace Slick put it, "If any musician represented that era, it was Jimi."

In mid–1966, former Yardbirds **guitarist Eric Clapton** *(center)* **formed Cream with Ginger Baker** *(left)* **on drums and Jack Bruce** *(right)* **on vocals and bass.** The power trio's second album, *Disraeli Gears*, and the single "Sunshine of Your Love" brought them international superstardom. With the 1968 release of *Wheels of Fire* and "White Room," Cream rose to the top of the rock pantheon, but they disbanded soon afterward. Although Baker and Bruce continued their careers, only Clapton was able to achieve substantial solo success.

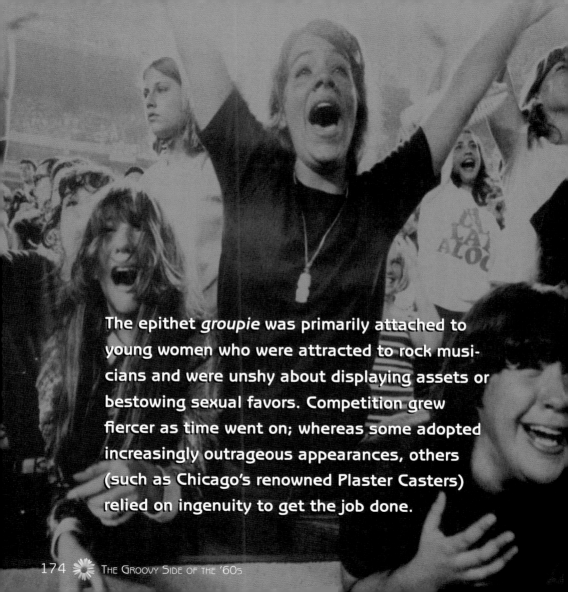

The epithet *groupie* was primarily attached to young women who were attracted to rock musicians and were unshy about displaying assets or bestowing sexual favors. Competition grew fiercer as time went on; whereas some adopted increasingly outrageous appearances, others (such as Chicago's renowned Plaster Casters) relied on ingenuity to get the job done.

At 8:00 P.M. on April 7, 1967, **San Francisco deejay Tom Donahue** at KPMX-FM inaugurated a new format of radio, which was later dubbed "progressive" or "free-form." This format featured long album cuts that broke commercial radio's prescribed three-minute barrier as

well as blocks of back-to-back sound in an unpredictable mix, in which trippy humor from the likes of the Firesign Theatre could crop up next to an obscure folk singer. The histrionics of AM disc jockeys were replaced by a mellow, laid-back delivery, and counterculture sponsors lined up to buy time. Within two years, over 2,000 similar stations across the United States had changed the music listening and buying experience of millions.

The First Super Bowl

This new American tradition started on January 15, 1967, when coach Vince Lombardi's **Green Bay Packers** squared off against the Kansas City Chiefs in Los Angeles's Memorial Coliseum. It was called the **Super Bowl,** and when it was all over, more than 60 million American TV viewers watched the Packers take the win, 35 to 10.

Poitier's Triple Threat

Already an Oscar winner for *Lilies of the Field*, Sidney Poitier exploded off the screen in 1967. Race riots were a fact of life, but Poitier was telling stories of reconciliation. *In the Heat of the Night* starred Poitier as Philadelphia detective Virgil Tibbs, forced to team with Rod Steiger's bigoted Mississippi sheriff on a murder investigation. Nominated for seven Oscars, including Best Picture, the

movie supplies a famous Poitier line: When asked how he is addressed by his Philadelphia colleagues, Poitier responds, "They call me *Mister* Tibbs."

The interracial love story *Guess Who's Coming to Dinner,* tame by 21st-century standards, was quite daring in its time.

Poitier was a doctor meeting his white girlfriend's parents, played by Katharine Hepburn and Spencer Tracy in their last picture together. Hepburn won the Oscar for Best Actress.

Poitier proved he could excel with lighter fare in *To Sir, with Love* **as a teacher entrusted with a London classroom of inner-city rebels.** His insistence that they learn to conduct themselves as human beings wins their loyalty and turns their lives around. The potential corniness factor was alleviated by Poitier's performance and the title song's delivery by English pop star Lulu.

Jefferson Airplane

This high-flying group, which helped define the San Francisco sound, was founded in 1965 by singer Marty Balin. The following year, during various personnel changes, **Grace Slick** joined up, bringing a couple of songs along with her: "Somebody To Love," written by her brother-in-law, and her own "White Rabbit." Both were included on Jefferson Airplane's first album, *Surrealistic Pillow*, which hit the Top Ten within months of its release.

Big Brother and the Holding Company

Big Brother was already established in San Francisco as a some-what sloppy blues-rock combo when Texas-born singer Janis Joplin joined in mid-'66 at the instigation of her friend, pro-moter Chet Helms. Her fiery wail and undeniable stage presence put the group on the map after its showstopping appearance at the Monterey Pop Festival.

Frustrated at what they saw as slow progress in the Civil Rights Movement, a number of African-Americans turned to more radical approaches. Bobby Seale and Huey Newton formed the militant Black Panther Party, which agitated for the right of African-American self-defense. **Stokely Carmichael,** leader of the Student Non-Violent Coordinating Committee (SNCC), had become increasingly radicalized and no longer supported interracial collaboration as espoused by Martin Luther King, Jr. More in tune with Malcolm X–style rhetoric, Carmichael coined the phrase "Black Power" and became

an outspoken advocate of black separatism and armed struggle. In 1967, Carmichael resigned from SNCC to take the position of prime minister in the Black Panther Party. Shortly after that, he left the Black Panthers as well, taking up the concept of pan-Africanism and moving to Guinea.

Ali Takes a Stand

Many people just didn't understand why a fighter didn't want to fight.

It wasn't the sweet science of boxing that heavyweight champ Muhammad Ali objected to—joining the U.S. Army to fight in Vietnam was where Ali drew the line. As a member of the Nation of Islam, Ali claimed conscientious objector status and refused military induction, saying, "I ain't got no quarrel with no Vietcong." He was subsequently stripped of his boxing crown and sentenced to five years in prison. The U.S. Supreme Court later overturned that conviction.

The Act You've Known
for All These Years

The Beatles were already acknowledged geniuses when they created *Sgt. Pepper's Lonely Hearts Club Band,* **the record that ushered in the age of album rock.** Partially inspired by the Beach Boys' *Pet Sounds* (and also LSD), this landmark also introduced several recording innovations that have since become standard, such as automatic double-tracking, which perfectly replicated a sound, and the speeding-up of vocals, known as "tweaking." But *Sgt. Pepper* was also **an album that could not easily be played live, signaling the end of the group's performing days.** During the Summer of Love, *Sgt. Pepper* permeated the very air, as if the entire globe was tuned in to one frequency. It won four Grammys, including Album of the Year, and topped a 2003 *Rolling Stone* poll of the "500 Greatest Albums of All Time." The most inventive rock group in the world had once again set the bar for their contemporaries and everyone that followed.

Some artists scorn commercialism—not Peter Max, whose celestial, semipsychedelic illustrations were plastered over everything from scarves and clocks to the Yellow Pages. Max's swirly, flowing lines were reminiscent of Art Nouveau, but his choice of vibrant candied colors was strictly '60s. Although Max didn't illustrate Yellow Submarine, as many erroneously believed, the animated movie did bear more than a passing resemblance to his style. By 1969, he had sold millions of posters and related products.

Underground comix—spelled with an *x* to differentiate this work from the more benign mainstream comic books—quickly found a place for themselves in the rest of the underground culture. The first, Robert Crumb's *Zap Comix* **No. 0, set the standard for a new wave of satiric cartoonists,** including S. Clay Wilson, Gilbert Shelton, Bill Griffith, and others. They were unafraid to depict their darkest, most visceral fantasies in dealing with subjects such as sex, drugs, rock, racism, and protest.

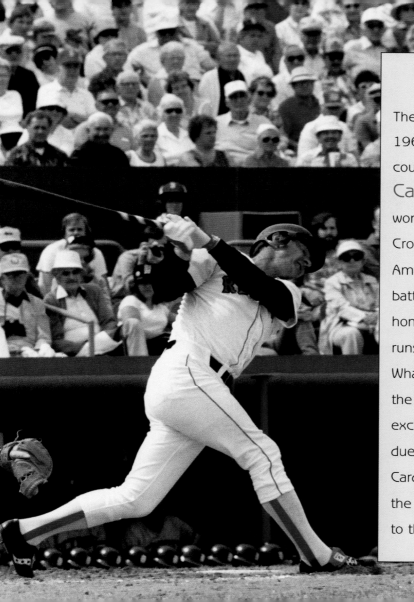

The Yaz

The left fielder for the 1967 Boston Red Sox could do no wrong— Carl Yastrzemski won baseball's Triple Crown, leading the American League in batting average (.326), home runs (44), and runs batted in (121). What's more, he led the Red Sox to an exciting World Series duel with the St. Louis Cardinals, who took the Series four games to three.

Aretha Franklin

"I Never Loved a Man (The Way I Love You)"

"Respect"

"Think"

"Chain of Fools"

"(You Make Me Feel Like) A Natural Woman"

Graduation Day

Plastics. That one word, eagerly whispered to recent graduate Benjamin Braddock (Dustin Hoffman) as the key to his future, summed up everything right about director Mike Nichols's **satirical take on alienated '60s youth.** The sharp script, Hoffman's adroit portrayal of post-adolescent drift, and an outstanding Simon and Garfunkel soundtrack (not to mention Anne Bancroft's Mrs. Robinson) helped make the film a must-see for young audiences and won Nichols an Academy Award.

What Color Are You Curious?

I Am Curious (Yellow), a film imported from Sweden, was a brief sensation for its full-frontal nudity and its frank discussion of sex, traits rarely seen at the time in American movies. The story of a female sociologist's survey of sexual mores was mostly confusing to American audiences who wanted to be considered *au courant*—and, of course, to see the good bits.

Nobody illuminated the dark underbelly of Los Angeles, or postadolescent angst, quite as vividly as **the Doors,** which became one of rock's most influential groups with "Light My Fire." The band innovatively replaced a bassist with organist Ray Manzarek, but its biggest draw was self-proclaimed Lizard King Jim Morrison—a galvanizing performer whose proclivity for drugs and alcohol eventually overshadowed his performances, helped lead to a 1969 arrest for indecent exposure onstage, and hastened his demise in 1971. The Doors released six albums during Morrison's brief lifetime, yet his persona as the ultimate Sexy Beast continues to thrive.

Thurgood Marshall, the grandson of a slave, became the first African-American to sit on the Supreme Court when he was sworn in on October 7, 1967. He would serve with distinction for 23 years. Denied entry to the University of Maryland as a young man because of his race, Marshall went on to graduate first in his class at Howard Law School. His first case as a lawyer involved successfully suing U of M to admit another African-American.

Abbie Hoffman, founder and leader of the "Youth International Party" (known as Yippies), promoted activism through anarchy. Hoffman, **Jerry Rubin,** and several

other Yippies created such a scene at the New York Stock Exchange on August 24, 1967, by tossing dollar bills onto the trading floor from the visitor's gallery, they nearly started a riot.

There's a Riot Going On

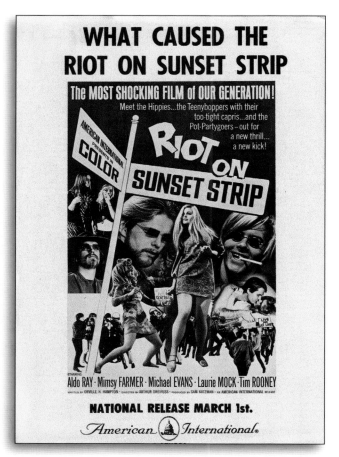

This 1967 exploitation flick, *Riot on Sunset Strip*, hoped to cash in on the real-life drama of youth clashing with the LAPD over turf rights to the Sunset Strip. Outside of campy awfulness, its primary value nowadays is the chance to see and hear garage-rockers such as the Standells, who sing their hit "Dirty Water," and Chocolate Watchband.

Period pieces don't come much more dated than *The Trip*, written by none other than Jack Nicholson and directed by horror schlockmeister Roger Corman. Corman claimed he took LSD before filming—just for research purposes, of course. Pre-*Easy Rider* stars Peter Fonda and Dennis Hopper provided further hipster credibility.

The Monterey Pop Festival

The Mamas and the Papas leader John Phillips and producer Lou Adler organized **the forerunner of all rock festivals,** a beatific three-day weekend in Monterey, California, on June 16–18, 1967. Paul McCartney was onboard as talent consultant, Otis Redding stepped in at the last minute at the suggestion of Rolling Stones' manager Andrew Loog Oldham, and at least 100,000—including a regally stoned Brian Jones—were in attendance for career-making performances from Jimi Hendrix and Janis Joplin, as well as appearances by the Who, Ravi Shankar, Simon and Garfunkel, the Grateful Dead, the Mamas and the Papas, Jefferson Airplane, Laura Nyro, the Byrds, and many more.

Just the Facts

There was hardly anything on '60s TV to match the unintentional camp value of deadpan LAPD Sgt. Joe Friday on the crime drama *Dragnet* asking for "just the facts, ma'am" in his doleful monotone. Friday was played by Jack Webb, who also produced and directed the series.

Dr. Richard Kimble, convicted of killing his own wife, knew the actual culprit was a mysterious one-armed man. Played by David Janssen, Kimble escaped custody and had to elude police while seeking the real murderer. Kids related to the innocent man wrongly accused, so *The Fugitive* kept on running—from 1963 to 1967.

Naturally High

Well, Sister Bertrille weighed less than 100 pounds, and her headpiece *did* have that winglike span. . . . Although Sister Bertrille's inadvertent airborne adventures caused her Reverend Mother no end of grief on *The Flying Nun*, anyone this adorable was always forgiven to soar once more. Former *Gidget* starlet Sally Field played the surfer-girl-turned-novice.

SILENT MAJORITY

It was no longer enough to hold an opinion silently— mindsets were now declared through buttons, small laminated badges, frequently worn *en masse*. The ubiquitous peace symbol and statements such as "Make Love, Not War" or "If It Moves, Fondle It" let everyone dig where you were at, man.

END WAR TAXES APRIL 15

FREEDOM RIDE CORE

ICA SALUTES

ARMSTRONG COLLINS ALDRIN
APOLLO XI JULY 1969
MEN ON THE MOON

FREE SPEECH F. S. M.

The Beatles had already conquered the music world—now they wanted the business world. Appearing on *The Tonight Show* (with Joe Garagiola guest-hosting for Johnny Carson) in May 1968, John and Paul announced the formation of **Apple Corps, a production company for records, films, electronics, publishing, and retailing**. They even opened a boutique, which went out of business very quickly.

History soon proved the Fab Four to be much better musicians than businesspeople.

During a mid-'60s concert tour of England, Bob Dylan allowed filmmaker D. A. Pennebaker an all-access *cinema verite* pass. The result was *Don't Look Back,* a landmark documentary film that quickly became required viewing for anyone interested in Dylan, the times that created him, popular music, or the nature of fame itself. One scene in which Dylan flashes cue cards during "Subterranean Homesick Blues" has been credited as the genesis of rock video.

Several publishers rejected Richard Brautigan's second novel, *Trout Fishing in America*, before it became an almost immediate best seller upon its eventual release in 1967. The book's gently satirical free-association style, which lamented the takeover of pastoral ideals by commercial interests, resonated with the counterculture and turned the author into something of a guru.

Like others his age, 21-year-old Jann Wenner worshiped rock 'n' roll. Unlike his peers, however, Wenner borrowed $7,500 from family and friends to launch *Rolling Stone* in November 1967. His stated goal was to make this publication "not just about music, but also the things and attitudes that the music embraces." The first issue cost 25 cents and sold only 5,000 of its 40,000-print run. That situation, however, soon improved.

ROLLING STONE

NOVEMBER 9, 1967
VOL. I, NO. 1

OUR PRICE:
TWENTY-FIVE CENTS

IN THIS ISSUE:

DONOVAN: An incredible Rolling Stone Interview, with this manchild of magic............Page 14

GRATEFUL DEAD: A photographic look at a rock and roll group after a dope bust..........Page 8

BYRD IS FLIPPED: Jim McGuinn kicks out David Crosby..............Page 4

RALPH GLEASON: The color bar on American television........Page 11

Recognize Private Gripeweed? He's actually John Lennon in Richard Lester's new film, How I Won the War. An illustrated special preview of the movie begins on page 16.

Tom Rounds Quits KFRC

Tom Rounds, KFRC Program Director, has resigned. No immediate date has been set for his departure from the station. Rounds quit to assume the direction of Charlatan Productions, an L.A. based film company experimenting in the contemporary pop film.

Rounds spent seven years as Program Director of KPOI in Hawaii before coming to San Francisco in 1966. He successfully effected the tight format which made KFRC the number one station in San Francisco.

Les Turpin, former program director of KGB in San Diego will replace Tom Rounds at KFRC. Turpin has spent the last year as a consultant in the Drake-Chenault programming service.

The new appointment could mean a tightening up of programming policies. Rounds liberalization of KFRC's play-list may well become more restricted.

THE HIGH COST OF MUSIC AND LOVE: WHERE'S THE MONEY FROM MONTEREY?

BY MICHAEL LYDON

A weekend of "music, love, and flowers" can be done for a song (plus cost) or can be done at a cost (plus songs). The Monterey International Pop Festival, a non-profit, charity event, was, despite its own protestations, of the second sort: a damn extravagant three days.

The Festival's net profit at the end of August, the last date of accounting, was $211,451. The costs of the weekend were $290,233. Had it not been for the profit from the sale of television rights to ABC-TV of $288,843, the whole operation would have ended up a neat $77,392 in the red.

The Festival planned to have all the artists, while in Monterey, submit ideas for use of the proceeds.

In the confusion the plan miscarried and the decision on where the profits should go has still not been finally made.

So far only $50,000 has definitely been been allocated to anyone: to a unit of the New York City Youth Board which will set up classes for many ghetto children to learn music on guitars donated by Fender. Paul Simon, a Festival governor, will personally over see the program.

Plans to give more money to the Negro College Fund for college scholarships is now being discussed; another idea is a sum between ten and twenty thousand for the Monterey Symphony.

However worthy these plans, they are considerably less daring and innovative than the projects mentioned in the spring: the Diggers, pop conferences, and any project which would "tend to further national interest in and knowledge and enjoyment of popular music." The present plans suggest that the Board of Governors, unable or unwilling to make their grandiose schemes reality, fell back on traditional charity.

The Board of Governors did decide that the money would be given out in a small number of large sums. This has meant, for instance, that the John Edwards Memorial Foundation, a folk music archive at the University of California at Los Angeles, had its small request overlooked.

In ironic fact, what happened at the Festival and its financial affairs looks in many ways like the traditional Charity Ball in hippie drag.

The overhead was high and the net was low. "For every dollar spent, there was a reason," says Derek Taylor, the Festival's PR man and one of its original officers.

Yet many of the Festival's expenses, however reasonable to Taylor, seem out of keeping with its announced spirit. The Festival management, with amateurish good will, lavished generosity on their friends.

• Producer Lou Adler was able to find a spot in the show for his own property, Johnny Rivers; Paul Simon for his friend, English folk singer Beverly; John Phillips for the Group Without A Name and Scott McKenzie. None of them had the musical

Airplane high, but no new LP release

Jefferson Airplane has been taking more than a month to record their new album for RCA Victor. In a recording period of five weeks only five sides have been completed. No definite release date has been set.

Their usual recording schedule in Los Angeles begins at 11:00 p.m. in the evening and extends through six or seven in the morning. When they're not in the studios, they stay at a fabulous pink mansion which rents for $5,000 a month. The Beatles stayed at the house on their last American tour.

The house has two swimming pools and a variety of recreational facilities. It's a small little paradise in the hills above Hollywood. Maybe suntans and guitars don't make it together.

status for an international pop music festival.

It is ironic that the Rivers and the rest appeared "free," but the money it cost the Festival to get them to Monterey and back, feed them, put them up (Beverly —Continued on Page 7

Influential Books of the Mid-'60s

The Crying of Lot 49, Thomas Pynchon

You Only Live Twice, Ian Fleming

The Arrogance of Power, J. William Fulbright

The Autobiography of Malcolm X, Alex Haley

Why We Can't Wait, Martin Luther King, Jr.

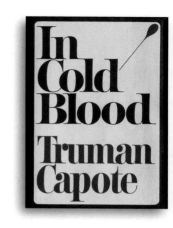

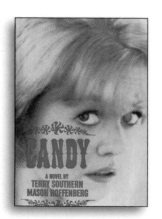

Understanding Media, Marshall McLuhan

The Painted Bird, Jerzy Kosinski

The Green Berets, Robin Moore

In Cold Blood, Truman Capote

Herzog, Saul Bellow

Against Interpretation, Susan Sontag

Candy, Terry Southern & Mason Hoffenberg

Eastern mysticism was a new discovery for Americans. The spiritual search for total conscious-ness, being at peace with one's self, embracing the art of Zen—all provided an alternative to well-established Christian beliefs for many. Gurus and yogis such as the Maharishi Mahesh Yogi, the Dalai Lama, and Sri Chinmoy, supported by famous followers that included the Beatles, Mike Love of the Beach Boys, and Donovan, offered guidance through the Hindu and Buddhist worlds of Hatha Yoga and Transcendental Meditation. For some, it was the direction they sorely needed.

Chapter 5

Born to Be Wild

An anthem for the age, Steppenwolf's "Born to Be Wild" was a
centerpiece of the counterculture
movie *Easy Rider.* The song
charted at No. 2 in 1968.

The '68 DNC Riots

The whole world was watching as the Democratic National Convention opened in Chicago in August 1968. President Lyndon Johnson refused to run, and an assassin's bullets had struck down Robert F. Kennedy, leaving the field to eventual nominee Vice President Hubert Humphrey and antiwar activist Senator Eugene McCarthy.

But the focus seemed to shift more toward what was going on outside the International Amphitheater rather than inside. **Throngs of antiwar protesters filled the public parks,** while a number of organized rallies called for an end to U.S. action in Vietnam. Tensions rose as police were pelted with rocks and bottles. They responded with viciousness, clubbing and dragging protesters, reporters, and photographers into waiting police wagons. More than 500 were arrested, and more than 200 police and demonstrators were injured.

Chicago Mayor Richard J. Daley came under attack for the brutal treatment by his police force. He inadvertently admitted the truth by saying, "The policeman isn't there to create disorder, the policeman is there to preserve disorder."

On *Cheap Thrills*, Big Brother and the Holding Company's No. 1 album, it was clear how deeply **Janis Joplin's voice was steeped in the blues.** Her ugly duckling persona morphed into that of a superstar on hits such as "Piece of My Heart," "Ball and Chain," and the Gershwin classic "Summertime." But the emotion that helped fuel Joplin's memorable performances also led to reckless behavior; by decade's turn, she had become one of rock 'n' roll's first major casualties.

Going Clean for Gene

Eugene McCarthy was a 52-year-old senator from Minnesota who **looked like your favorite uncle.** He entered the race for the 1968 Democratic presidential nomination with a **strong opposition to the Vietnam War,** and his impressive showing in the New Hampshire

primary against President Johnson convinced LBJ not to stand for reelection.

Many of McCarthy's supporters were typically long-haired, tie-dyed hippies. The **"Clean for Gene"** campaign was born when, realizing a conservative image was more effective, the flower-child followers cut their hair, shaved, and put on suits and dresses. McCarthy didn't win the nomination in the end, but his voice for peace was still actively heard.

GIRLS SAY YES

to boys who say NO

Proceeds from the sale of this poster go to The Draft Resistance.

Offering a different slant on the 1968 antiwar and **antidraft movement,** folk singer and activist Joan Baez, along with her sisters Mimi Fariña and Pauline Marden, accented the message with the leggy lure of their feminine charms.

The Poor People's Campaign

Before his assassination in April 1968, Dr. Martin Luther King, Jr., revealed a plan to **balance economic hardships** for the underprivileged in America. With the direction of the Southern Christian Leadership Conference, the Poor People's Campaign sought to focus attention on poverty through nonviolent civil disobedience.

But King's death left the movement stalled at the starting gate. Protesters journeyed to Washington, but they received little reaction from lawmakers, and the campaign was closed by June.

When the flower-power-themed rock musical *Hair* moved from Joe Papp's Public Theatre to Broadway, it became the first off-Broadway show to make it to the Great White Way. Subtitled *The American Tribal Love Rock Musical*, the show made the transition with its outrageousness—including onstage nudity—intact. Depending on your point of view, this was either a vulgarian invasion of one of the last unsullied bastions of culture or a cynical co-opting of hippie ideals for profit. *Hair* received mixed reviews yet ran on Broadway for more than four years.

Comedy team **Dick and Tommy Smothers** hosted an hour of comedy and music on CBS, but the show, begun in February '67, gradually grew

more audacious in its satire and musical guests, which included blacklisted folksinger Pete Seeger singing "Waist Deep in the Big Muddy" and a literally explosive appearance by the Who (it also launched the career of then-writer Steve Martin). The brothers became a First Amendment cause célèbre in April 1969 when CBS canceled *The Smothers Brothers Comedy Hour* after ongoing battles over its content.

Rowan and Martin's Laugh-In first appeared as an NBC special but quickly took its place in the regular schedule. Fast-paced and hip, it **came direct from "beautiful downtown Burbank."** Hosted by the stand-up team of Dan Rowan and Dick Martin, *Laugh-In* featured a large cast of regulars, including Lily Tomlin and Goldie Hawn, and cameo appearances from the biggest stars in the business. The show

popularized the phrases "You bet your sweet bippy," "Here come de judge," "Very interesting," and many others. During the 1968 presidential campaign, even Dick Nixon dropped in to say, "Sock it to me."

Out of This World

Bookended by scenes of skin-prickling awe, director Stanley Kubrick's *2001: A Space Odyssey*, which he wrote with Arthur C. Clarke, was marketed as "the ultimate trip" to a psychedelically conversant audience. This dazzling epic became one of 1968's top-grossing films by intellectually challenging viewers as no sci-fi adventure ever had. After the fear and pity elicited by HAL, the spaceship computer gone mad, "Daisy Bell," the song about a bicycle built for two, never sounded quite the same.

The Beatles had proved themselves to be movie stars in *A Hard Day's Night* and *Help!,* but **could they compete against Popeye and Mickey Mouse?** The boys found themselves in Pepperland when the full-length cartoon ***Yellow Submarine*** was released late in 1968. They were pitted against the villainous Blue Meanies, but of course, multiple musical moments featured classic and new Beatles tunes. The Fab Four made a surprise live-action appearance at the film's end.

RFK

He was young, vibrant, enthusiastic—just as his brother had been only eight years before.

Robert Francis Kennedy had originally balked at running for the Democratic presidential nomination in 1968, but he quickly realized there was a large faction of America that simply did not want to be involved in Vietnam. After entering the race, Kennedy began to win Democratic primaries. He continued to gain momentum toward the White House by winning South Dakota and California on June 4. Celebrating his victory at a late-night press conference in Los Angeles's Ambassador Hotel, RFK was gunned down by Sirhan Sirhan, putting an end to Kennedy's life and the hopes many Americans had placed in it.

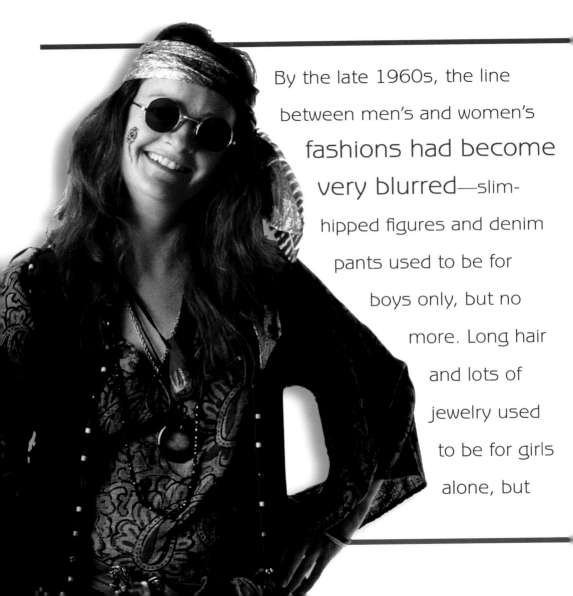

By the late 1960s, the line between men's and women's fashions had become very blurred—slim-hipped figures and denim pants used to be for boys only, but no more. Long hair and lots of jewelry used to be for girls alone, but times had changed. Fresh new clothes were out—**worn out, ragged, sloppy styles were in,** and psychedelic tie-dye fashions reflected the increasing popularity of mind-bending drugs. Men grew their hair—on their heads and on their faces—and the longer, the better. Head bands and "granny" glasses completed the look of "nonconformity"—the look everyone wanted.

Leading journalist and best-selling author Tom Wolfe penned *The Electric Kool-Aid Acid Test* in 1968, documenting the cross-country bus trip of psychedelic pioneer Ken Kesey and his Merry Pranksters. The book explored the wild world of the hippie culture, free love, and mind-altering drugs.

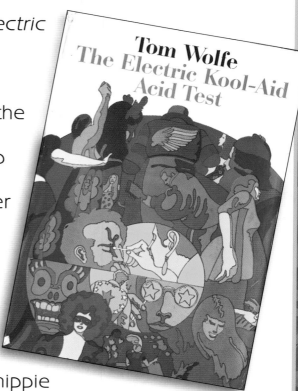

Militant students began demonstrating at **Colum-bia University** in New York City in late April 1968 when it became known that the university was conducting research for war interests. The protest quickly grew ugly, as school **buildings were overtaken and school officials held hostage for 24 hours.** An estimated 1,000 students ran rampant over the school grounds. More than 1,000 NYC police came in to put the rebellion down.

School was out for the year.

Women's Lib

Activists for women's issues, such as Kate Millet and Ti-Grace Atkinson, made their points crystal clear in the late 1960s: Gender differences are social, not biological, in nature. Women wanted to achieve equality in the job market and in the homes of America. Feminist leaders, including Germaine Greer and Gloria Steinem, supported the campaign against female oppression.

Many outspoken members of the feminist movement sought to free themselves from what they considered to be "shackles"—bras and girdles. The 1968 Miss America Pageant became the protest scene for the "Freedom Trash Can," a receptacle for all the undergarments, cosmetics, and high-heeled shoes from which women chose to free themselves.

The King
Returns

Elvis Presley had taken a mighty fall since his rockin' heyday of the 1950s, overshadowed by fresher music from younger '60s groups. By the mid-'60s, he seemed content to star in movies—mostly empty save for his few musical moments. But a televised NBC special on December 3, 1968, brought a leather-clad Elvis back into America's living rooms and proved that **this King was far from dead.**

Pierre Cardin and Rudi Gernreich both received credit for inventing **unisex fashion,** intended to be sexless, any-gender outfits for the space-age '60s.

It was a contrast of creeds: Two American track stars, **Tommie Smith** and **John Carlos**, **raised their fists defiantly as a symbol of Black Power** when they accepted their medals at the 1968 Summer

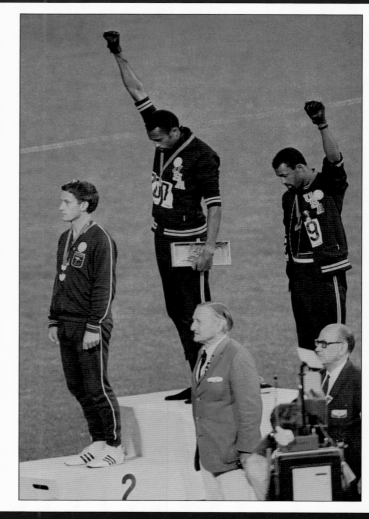

Olympics in Mexico City. At another venue, however, U.S.

heavyweight gold medalist George Foreman **raised an**

American flag in triumph and pride.

Running for Office

Lyndon Johnson's decision not to run for reelection, along with the assassination of front-running Democratic candidate Bobby Kennedy and the presence of third-party opponent George Wallace, led to a squeaky tight race for the 1968 presidency.

Republican Richard Nixon, who vowed never to run again in the early '60s, ran a strong race against Vice President Hubert Humphrey. While American Independent Party candidate Wallace did well in the South, carrying nearly two-thirds of the popular vote in Alabama and Mississippi, the final result found Nixon edging Humphrey by a slim margin of less than 1 million votes out of more than 72 million cast.

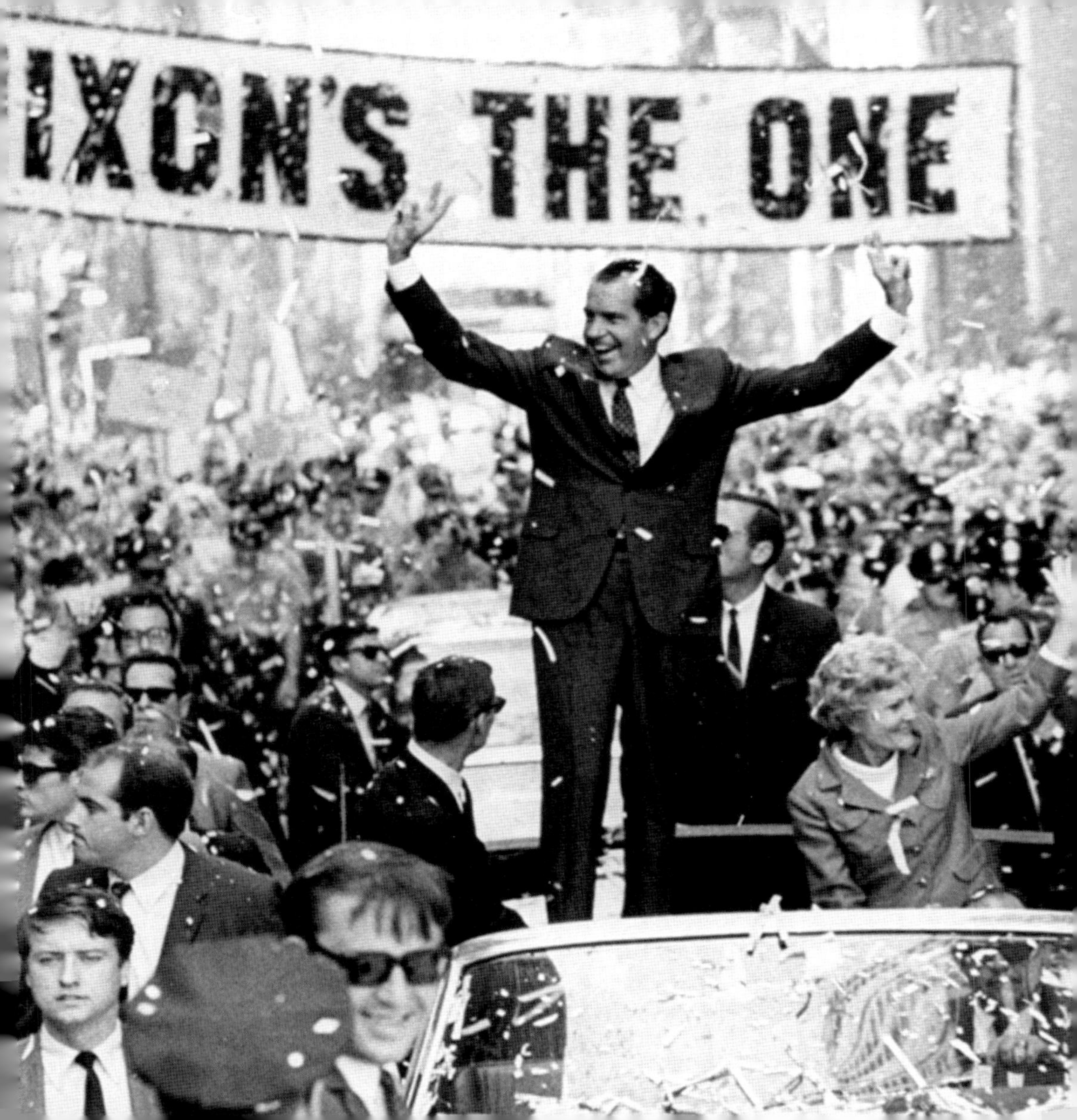
IXON'S THE ONE

A Silent Majority?

When Richard Nixon became president, he inherited a very unpopular war in Southeast Asia. In addressing the American public on November 9, 1969, he claimed the loud voice of antiwar protesters was a minority and called upon "the great silent majority" of Americans to support his path of continued conflict in Vietnam.

Your Friendly Neighborhood Spider-Man

By 1968, student unrest could be found every-where, even on the cover of your favorite comic book. Writer Stan Lee and artist Steve Ditko had created Spider-Man in 1962 for Marvel Comics, making him an ordinary guy with extraordinary powers. Readers could identify with the character, whose amazing abilities didn't protect him from debt, girl trouble, or any of the other annoyances of everyday life. As much as possible with spider-powers, he was a part of the real world, so in the late '60s, he encountered "Crisis on Campus!" This storyline wasn't as radical as John Romita's image may suggest, for the students are agitating merely for a new dorm building. But the tension depicted here accurately reflected the current college zeitgeist.

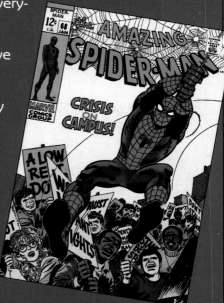

Charlton Heston, dangling from a net wearing only a loincloth, cursed those "damned, dirty apes." The hit movie ***Planet of the Apes*** featured an upside-down world in which monkeys kept humans in cages. Heston portrayed a sulking space traveler stuck on the simian planet—only to find out he had been home all along.

Daughter of the great actor Henry Fonda, sex kitten Jane romped in the **"so bad, it's good"** space saga *Barbarella*. The story of this futuristic damsel in distress, directed by Fonda's husband, Roger Vadim, was racy, silly, and campy. Few viewers could forget the zero-gravity striptease Jane performs in the opening credits.

They were the dominant hurlers in their respective leagues in 1968: Tall and powerful, St. Louis Cardinal **Bob Gibson** stifled hitters with a 1.12 earned run average, the lowest since 1914. Detroit Tigers' ace **Denny McClain** compiled

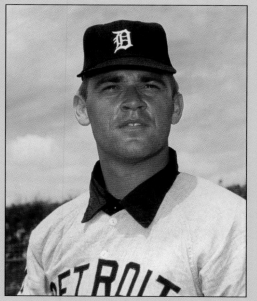

an amazing win-loss record of 31 and 6 in the same year, the first pitcher to win 30 or more since 1934. Both players led their teams to a showdown in the 1968 World Series, where the Tigers defeated the Cards in seven games.

There had never been anything like the **Big Mac** in fast-food hamburgers. McDonald's introduced the oversize sandwich after successfully testing this brainchild of an owner/operator in Pennsylvania. What a filling concept—two all-beef patties, special sauce, lettuce, cheese, pickles, onions, on a sesame-seed bun.

The Chicago Seven

Charged with conspiracy and inciting a riot at the 1968 Democratic National Convention, these eight men received a high-profile trial that quickly devolved into a circus. When Bobby Seale was separated from the group to receive his own trial, the remaining defendants became known as the Chicago Seven. All were found guilty of contempt of court—verdicts that were overturned on appeal when a higher court ruled that the Chicago Seven had not received a fair trial.

Jerry Rubin, Abbie Hoffman, Thomas Hayden, Rennie Davis, Bobby Seale, Lee Weiner, John Froines, and David Dellinger

Soul Brother No. 1

As the Civil Rights Movement surged forward with increased urgency, black recording artists began to employ more messages in their music that the personal was political. One of the first was Soul Brother No. 1, **James Brown,** a man whose talent and determination had already triumphed over institutionalized racism. He took another giant step forward in October 1968 with "Say It Loud (I'm Black and I'm Proud)," an assertive funk anthem that became a million-selling symbol of self-esteem.

Otis

The son of a Baptist minister, Otis Redding made little progress in the world of rhythm and blues during the mid–'60s. But a powerful and gripping performance at the Monterey Pop Festival demonstrated what Otis was all about. Sadly, his promising career vanished in a plane crash in December 1967. Yet his voice lived on in his million-selling hit, "(Sittin' on) The Dock of the Bay," which hit No. 1 in February 1968.

Diahann Carroll made history in 1968 when she became the first female African-American to star in her own TV show, NBC's *Julia.* As Julia Baker, Carroll played the single mother of a five-year-old boy; she had lost her husband in Vietnam. *Julia* finished in the Top Ten for the 1968 season and lasted for two more.

Cops in Paradise

In **Hawaii Five-O,** Steve McGarrett, played by Jack Lord, ran the special unit of the Hawaii state police amid sandy beaches and sprawling palm trees. McGarrett sealed criminals' fates by ordering costar James MacArthur as Danny Williams to "Book 'em, Danno." The Ventures took the show's instrumental theme song to No. 4 on the record charts.

Noted for its memorable high-speed car chase scenes, *Bullitt*, along with its star Steve McQueen, left movie audiences breathless. As tough police detective Frank Bullitt, McQueen did his own stunt driving in a hot Ford Mustang. His pursuit of a Dodge Charger reached 110 miles per hour on the hilly streets of San Francisco.

STEVE McQUEEN AS 'BULLITT'
A SOLAR PRODUCTION

The word 'cop' isn't written all over him—something more puzzling is.

ROBERT VAUGHN

JACQUELINE BISSET·DON GORDON·ROBERT DUVALL·SIMON OAKLAND·NORMAN FELL

Noted baby doctor **Benjamin Spock,** along with peace activist and Yale chaplain Dr. William Sloane Coffin, found themselves in hot water with the U.S. government in early 1968. A federal grand jury indicted them on charges of "conspiracy to counsel, aid, and abet draft resistance." Initially found guilty, their verdict was overturned on appeal.

Paul Krassner

An innovator in the world of under-ground journalism, Krassner edited *The Realist* magazine throughout the decade, combining biting satire, insight-ful interviews, and serious articles with bawdy cartoons and a clear counterculture attitude. In his spare time, he edited Lenny Bruce and helped found the Yippies.

Produced by horror master William Castle, *Rosemary's Baby* left moviegoers in shock. Starring Mia Farrow, John Cassavetes, and Ruth Gordon and directed by Roman Polanski, the film told the story of a young New York City couple who may end up with a "devil" of a newborn child.

Never Trust Anyone Over 30

When 24-year-old rock star Max Frost becomes president in the counterculture film **Wild in the Streets,** everyone over 30 has reason to worry: They are forced into retirement homes where LSD is mandatory and inmates are ordered to "mellow out." This movie dramatized the sentiment that you should never trust anyone over 30.

Jackie Kennedy Onassis

The nation may have lost a president in 1963, but Jackie Kennedy lost her husband. While the country mourned, she took her children and moved to New York City. And as the people of America recovered, so did Jackie. She met and married Greek shipping tycoon Aristotle "Ari" Onassis, nearly 30 years older and several inches shorter than the 5-foot 7-inch widow. The **general public,** as well as members of the Kennedy family, were stunned—this wasn't how a charismatic former first lady and widow of a slain president should carry on.

She became **known to the media as "Jackie O,"** and stories and photos of shopping sprees, nude sunbathing, and marital difficulties circulated. But the couple remained married until the mid–1970s, when Ari died of pneumonia. Jackie returned to New York City, becoming a book editor for Doubleday Publishing. She died from lymphoma in May 1994, still an icon of '60s American royalty.

Even the cops had cool kids on the force. Television's **The Mod Squad** was comprised of Afro'ed Linc (Clarence Williams III), pretty-boy Pete (Michael Cole), and California-girl Julie (Peggy Lipton, who won a Golden Globe for her role). The characters all had minor criminal records when they were recruited as undercover agents, sans guns or badges, with a directive to bust adults preying upon the young. The show aired for five years after its hit debut in September 1968.

Whole Earth Catalog

It wasn't your typical "Holiday Wish Book."

First published in 1968 by biologist Stewart Brand, the *Whole Earth Catalog* offered an eclectic assortment of books, maps, classes, tools, prices, and suppliers. A shopper could find hiking shoes or gardening tools. The catalog was an "alternative" resource for socially and ecologically minded buyers.

Chapter 6

Let the Sunshine In

The **Fifth Dimension** sat on top of the charts for six straight weeks in 1969 with "Aquarius/Let the Sunshine In," a medley of two songs from the popular rock musical *Hair*.

By the Time We Got to Woodstock

Woodstock actually took place on Max Yasgur's dairy farm in nearby Bethel, New York, starting at 5:07 P.M. on August 15, 1969. It all comes back in kalei-

doscopic fragments of imagery now, this musical and sociopolitical event that lent its name to a generation: **Endless traffic jams** on the highway, with helicopters becoming the only way in or out. Food airlifted in from Newburgh's Stewart Air Force Base. First the sun beating down and then the rains, providing mud and an excuse for nudity and communal bathing holes. Freeloaders surging in and trampling the fence, unexpectedly making it a "free" concert. Bad acid trips flocking to the "Freak-Out Tent." Three fatalities and several births. "What we have in mind is breakfast in bed for 500,000" (there had never been a concert for even 50,000 before). Jimi Hendrix, at third day's dawning, playing a distorted electric version of "The Star-Spangled Banner." Ravi Shankar, Joan Baez, Richie Havens, and Arlo Guthrie. Sly and the Family Stone, Creedence Clearwater Revival, and

Jefferson Airplane. The Band, Joe Cocker, and Ten Years After. Country Joe and the Fish, Santana, and the debut of Crosby, Stills, Nash, and Young. Janis Joplin, the Grateful Dead, and the Who refusing to go on unless paid in advance. A sea of young humanity proving—for one brief shining moment—that despite hardship, hunger, and fatigue, we all really could get along.

Inauguration Day

About 10,000 citizens lined the streets of Washington, D.C., for Richard M. Nixon's first inauguration in January 1969; roughly a tenth or more of that number were protestors who pelted the President's limousine with beer cans, rocks, and ink-filled balloons while shouting antiwar epithets ("Four more years of death"). Protestors were outnumbered two-to-one by military troops.

To the Moon

The United States won the race to the moon in July 1969. Using the massive Saturn V booster designed specifically for the moon launch, astronauts Neil Armstrong and Edwin "Buzz" Aldrin separated

their lunar lander, nicknamed *Eagle*, from Michael Collins, who stayed aboard *Columbia*, the command module. As America held its breath, the lunar module, or LM, made its way toward the surface of the moon.

Part of JFK's legacy was realized when Neil Armstrong stepped off the ladder of the LM and became the first human to set foot on a terrestrial object other than Earth. Armstrong's words, **"That's one small step for man . . . one giant leap for mankind,"** were beamed back to a gasping world via live television. Aldrin joined him shortly, and the two duck-walked their way across the dry and dusty Sea of Tranquility. The universe had just become a bit smaller.

See the U.S.A.

Hippie-freak paranoia peaked with the release of *Easy Rider*, in which "a man went looking for America and couldn't find it anywhere." It was actually two men: **Peter Fonda and Dennis Hopper,** who co-

authored the Academy Award–nominated screenplay with *Candy* author Terry Southern. The stars played free spirits who unwittingly threatened denizens of a land with little tolerance for cultural change. After

appearing in movies and on TV for a decade, Jack Nicholson gave a performance that made everyone sit up and take notice. Record producer Phil Spector had a bit part as a drug dealer, and the rock band Steppenwolf lent a charge to the soundtrack. Hollywood suddenly had to rethink its youth game plan.

Cinematographer Haskell Wexler blurred the lines between fact and fiction with **Medium Cool,** shot partially during the riots of the '68 Chicago convention. Wexler mixed documentary-style techniques with scripted dialogue to create an indelible portrait—not only of his protagonist, a detached cameraman (Robert Forster) coming to a belated awakening, but of an America in political turmoil. Wexler demonstrated how readily an audience can be manipulated through the power of visual imagery.

Although the origins of **com-munal living** go back to the 2nd century B.C., the concept seemed brand new again in the '60s. The well-being of the collective was put above that of individual members, who **might share everything from finances to bed partners to the raising of food and/or families.** Communes could be rural or urban, spiritual or anarchistic, egalitarian or authoritarian. The abiding basic principle was "from each according to his ability, to each according to his need."

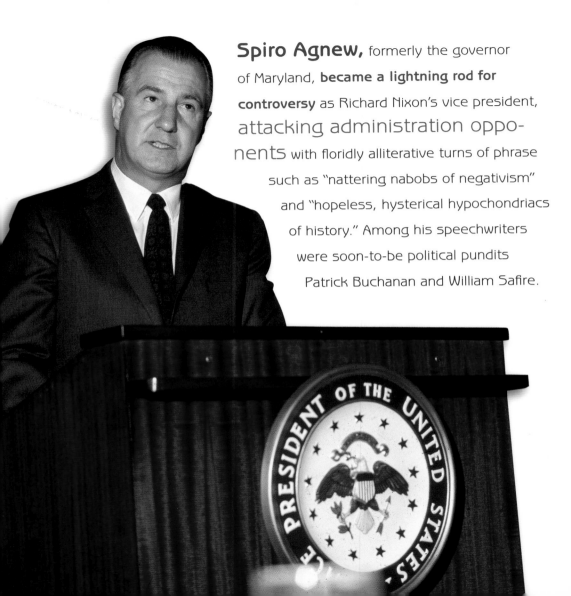

Spiro Agnew, formerly the governor of Maryland, **became a lightning rod for controversy** as Richard Nixon's vice president, attacking administration opponents with floridly alliterative turns of phrase such as "nattering nabobs of negativism" and "hopeless, hysterical hypochondriacs of history." Among his speechwriters were soon-to-be political pundits Patrick Buchanan and William Safire.

Real life calls for real taste.
For the taste of your life—it's Coca-Cola.
Here and now.

Coke
TRADE-MARK ®

Coca-Cola
TRADE-MARK ®

It's the real thing.
Coke.

What could be more American than the combination of Coca-Cola and marketing? The soft drink was sloganeering even upon its 1886 launch with the simple "Drink Coca-Cola." By 1929, it had become "the Pause That Refreshes." But modern times required something more straightforward and authentic. In 1969, Coke became "the Real Thing."

Time magazine first coined the phrase **op art** in 1964 to characterize **a format that exploited the way in which the eye processes information to create illusionary, sometimes dizzying, artwork.** The concept was significantly popularized through a show at New York's Museum of Modern Art, which included Hungarian-born French painter **Victor Vasarely** and the British Bridget Riley.

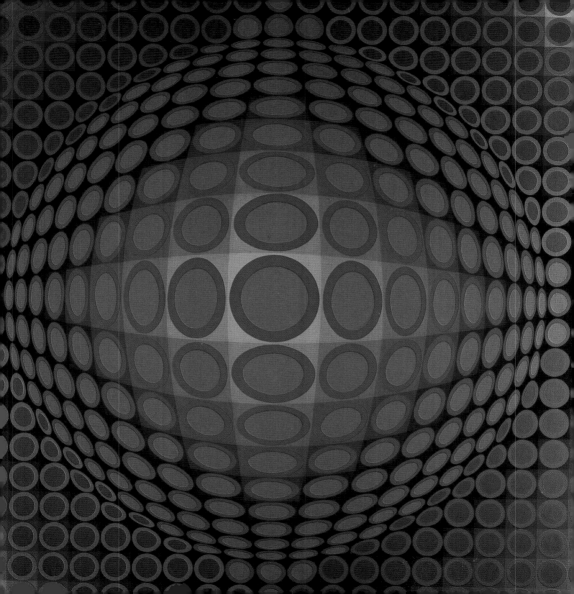

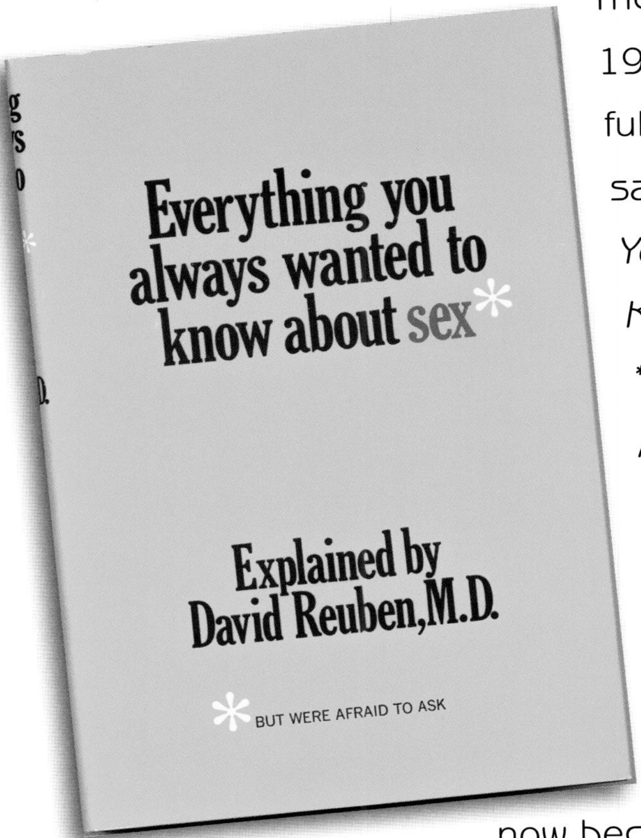

The title of one of 1969's most successful books seemed to say it all: *Everything You Always Wanted to Know About Sex* *but Were Afraid to Ask.* **The "sexual revolution" was well underway**— what had previously been unspeakable now became common currency, and no one wanted to be left behind. Sex

Everything you
always wanted to
know about sex*

Explained by
David Reuben, M.D.

* BUT WERE AFRAID TO ASK

books were everywhere. Philip Roth's novel

Portnoy's Complaint provided the sexually frank exploits of the unappeasable Alexander Portnoy. *The Sensuous Woman* was a self-help manual penned by an anonymous author who used only the coy initial *J*, proving that perhaps some things were still resistant to change.

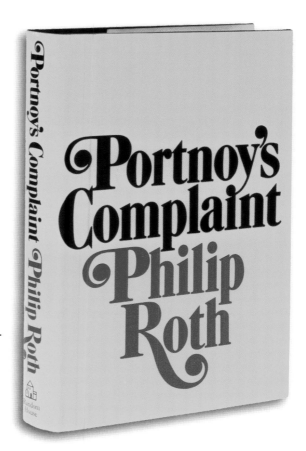

On March 12, 1969, Beatle Paul McCartney broke many hearts by marrying New York photographer Linda Eastman in a simple service at London's Marylebone registry office. None of the other Beatles attended the ceremony—years later, Paul said he couldn't remember whether he'd invited them or not.

Not to be outdone, on March 20, John Lennon and Yoko Ono were married in Gibraltar near Spain. Again, no other members of the band were present—George Harrison commented that he was so clueless, he'd had to buy the record "The Ballad of John and Yoko," which

related the couple's story. The couple traveled to Amsterdam for a (fully clothed) "bed-in" to promote peace, which was later repeated in Montreal.

In late October, rumors—spurred by a Michigan college newspaper—began to fly that McCartney had actually been dead since 1966, replaced by a doppelgänger. Many supposed tip-offs, so it was said, could be found in the cover art for *Sgt. Pepper, Abbey Road*, and

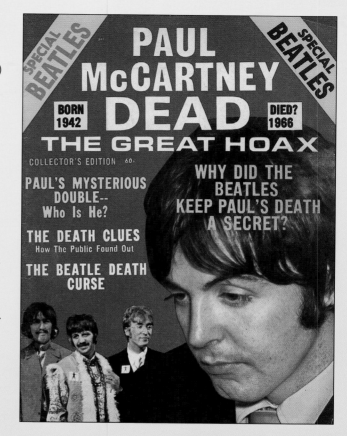

Magical Mystery Tour. All of Apple Records' denials were in vain. John Lennon flatly declared: "Paul McCartney couldn't die without the world knowing it. . . . It's just insanity—but it's a great plug for *Abbey Road*."

Student Unrest

An SDS rally at noon on April 9, 1969, erupted into the **seizure of Harvard's University Hall** when hundreds of demonstrators ejected the administration. The group issued its list of demands, which included the abolishment of ROTC (Reserve Officer Training Corps) recruitment from the campus. The following dawn **400 police staged a raid and arrested between 200 and 300 demonstrators; dozens were injured.** The day after that, students staged a strike, enlisting the support of some faculty. The strike ended two weeks later with the establishment of a student-monitored black studies program and a vote to make ROTC an "extracurricular" activity.

The **University of California campus at Berkeley** had already been a political tinderbox for at least three years when **student activists attempted to take over a vacant plot for a "People's Park"** in May 1969. When the university tried to fence off the land, a protest rally was assembled, and Governor Ronald Reagan responded with the National Guard. The situation escalated rapidly after that: Tear gas was sprayed while protestors threw rocks and bottles. In the end, more than a hundred were hospitalized, at least a dozen with bullet wounds. One officer was stabbed, and a bystander was killed by police gunfire.

Broadway Joe

Quarterback "Broadway Joe" Namath broke the clean-cut sports-hero mold in 1965 after the New York Jets (of the perennially second-place American Football League) signed him to a three-year, $427,000 contract. This Rookie of the Year had shaggy hair, glamorous charisma, and an extraordinary "rocket arm"; he loved football, women, booze, and stardom. Yet Namath's rebel ways didn't stop him from leading the Jets to a surprise victory over the Baltimore Colts in the 1969 Super Bowl.

The Miracle Mets

Most of 1969 America expected baseball's Chicago Cubs to finish first in the National League. Few paid any attention to the New York Mets, in only their eighth year of existence. But a complete Cub meltdown, coupled with an incredible finish by the Mets of 38 wins out of 49 games, led to a World Series showdown between the winning "Miracle Mets" and the Baltimore Orioles. Keeping the miracle alive, the Mets won the series in five games.

Hare Krishna

Many young people became adherents of the peace-and-love Krishna philosophy popularized in the West by Indian guru Srila Prabhupada. Shaven-headed devotees in flowing saffron robes rattled tambourines and chanted "Hare Krishna" on city streets and, more and more, in airports, seeking to illuminate oft-uninterested passersby.

Arlo Guthrie, Woody's son, recorded an amusing account of being busted by "Officer Obie" for littering and his later experiences with the draft board called "Alice's Restaurant Massacree." When it became a movie starring Arlo himself, the legend of Alice's Restaurant, where you can get anything you want, was forever established.

One Bunch

Director Sam Peckinpah may have wanted to present the final word on the mythically heroic Wild West. Now thought to be a classic, upon its release *The Wild Bunch* was highly controversial for the bloodily realistic battles that inevitably reminded critics and audiences of the carnage then taking place in Vietnam. A botched robbery leads the Bunch, headed by William Holden, on a flight to Mexico that culminates in a nihilistic rock-and-a-hard-place finale.

Another Bunch

The Brady Bunch was a brood of a different kind. Producer Sherwood Schwartz had originally wanted to hire up-and-coming actor Gene Hackman to play Mike Brady.

After **fashion designer Yves Saint Laurent** left Dior in 1961 to open his own couture house, he was inspired by young Parisiennes to create clothing that reflected real life, thus elevating pantsuits, pea jackets, boots, and sweaters to the runway. He also introduced see-through dresses and evening tuxedos for women.

Rudi Gernreich and Yves Saint Laurent each popularized **see-through clothing,** giving body-confident women—usually the young and bold—a chance to flaunt their assets.

Dr. Thomas Harris believed that most of us decide in childhood that we are not as good as others, an attitude which can create a "negative life position" and subsequent unhappiness. Transactional Analysis was the theory that helped sell millions of copies of his self-help tome, *I'm OK—You're OK*.

Angela Davis was a 25-year-old philosophy professor at UCLA in 1969 when she was **fired due to her membership in the American branch of the Communist Party.** When a lawsuit challenged the UC Board of Regents' decision, the state Supreme Court ruled the action illegal. Davis had continued to teach during the lawsuit, but she went underground the next year after making the FBI's Most Wanted list for allegedly supplying a gun used in a deadly shootout at the Marin County Courthouse. Tried and acquitted for that crime, Davis later joined the faculty at UC Santa Cruz.

A college basketball star at UCLA, **Lew Alcindor** led his 1967, '68, and '69 teams to a combined overall record of 88 and 2. At 7 feet, 2 inches tall, Alcindor dominated the game and was the number-one NBA draft pick in 1969. Converting to Islam in 1971, he changed his name to Kareem Abdul-Jabbar.

As a prisoner of war in 1945, Kurt Vonnegut, Jr., witnessed the fire-bombing destruction of Dresden, Germany, by the Allies. In the introduction to his novel *Slaughterhouse-Five: or The Children's Crusade* 24 years later, he wrote, "There is nothing intelligent to say about a massacre." This time-travel fable and its strong antiwar message was a best seller. It became newsworthy again in 1982, when the Supreme Court overturned a local school board's ban of the book in a case brought by teenage students.

Two Different Cowboy Pictures

Butch Cassidy and the Sundance Kid was 1969's most popular film, not least due to the chemistry between the two leads. Paul Newman and Robert Redford portrayed the wisecracking Old West outlaw buddies who flee to Bolivia after a thwarted train heist. Director George Roy Hill took a relatively light-handed approach to this based-on-real-life tale, resulting in big box office and several Oscars.

Originally rated X for nudity and adult themes that were considered shocking in 1969, *Midnight Cowboy* would later be downgraded to R as audience tolerance grew. Dustin Hoffman erased his clean-cut turn in *The Graduate* by playing derelict "Ratso" Rizzo, befriended by Jon Voight (who was nominated for an Oscar) as gigolo-wannabe Joe Buck. Shot on location in New York City by British Director John Schlesinger, this unflinching look at society's bottom-feeders and their unfulfilled dreams won the Academy Award for Best Picture.

On November 15, 1969, more than two million people around the country reportedly took part in demonstrations against America's ongoing involvement in Vietnam. Washington, D.C., saw the most massive turnout, with estimates of anywhere from a quarter- to a half-million protestors (officials gave varying accounts). This **"Peace**

Moratorium"

occurred directly after a 40,000-strong "March Against Death" past the White House, in which each participant carried the name of a soldier who had died in the conflict. Those in attendance included three U.S. senators, the widow of Dr. Martin Luther King, Jr., and composer Leonard Bernstein. **Vice President Spiro Agnew responded by accusing the protestors of being Communist dupes.** The

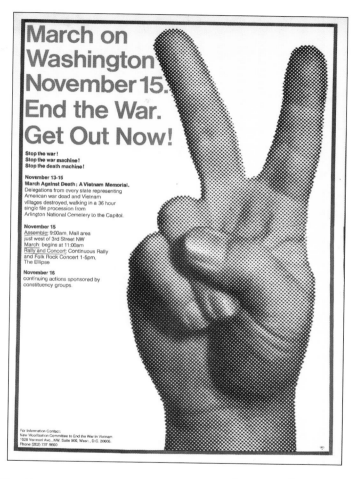

March on Washington November 15. End the War. Get Out Now!

Stop the war!
Stop the war machine!
Stop the death machine!

November 13-15
March Against Death: A Vietnam Memorial.
Delegations from every state representing American war dead and Vietnam villages destroyed, walking in a 36 hour single file procession from Arlington National Cemetery to the Capitol.

November 15
Assemble: 9:00am. Mall area just west of 3rd Street NW
March: begins at 11:00am
Rally and Concert: Continuous Rally and Folk Rock Concert 1-5pm, The Ellipse

November 16
continuing actions sponsored by constituency groups.

For Information Contact:
New Mobilization Committee to End the War in Vietnam.
1029 Vermont Ave., NW, Suite 900, Wash., D.C. 20005.
Phone (202) 737-8600

Washington march came off without violence and remains the largest such gathering in the nation's history.

Tang Temporarily Displaces Real Orange Juice

The Gemini Astronauts drank Tang...like this.
You can drink it from a glass.

The Gemini Astronauts drank Tang in space. Tang has been carried on the Gemini flights ... including the 7-6 rendezvous mission. Tang is the instant breakfast drink with more vitamin C and A — more than orange juice, tomato juice or any juice. And Tang with natural orange flavor is the breakfast drink your whole family will go for. Mix them some Tang tomorrow morning.

A powdered citrus-flavored beverage called **Tang** had actually been on supermarket shelves since 1959, but after General Mills instituted a canny '65 ad blitz touting this "drink of the astronauts" (who, after all, didn't have much choice in the beverage department), children everywhere began clamoring for the bright orange stuff.

A slender cigarette called **Virginia Slims,** designed to be a fashion accessory specifically for women, was launched in 1968 with the semi-feminist slogan "You've come a long way, baby." *Baby* was added only after a poll determined it didn't offend potential consumers.

In 1915, Mrs. Cynthia Robinson was caught smoking in the cellar behind the preserves. Although she was 34, her husband sent her straight to her room.

It's different now. Now there's a slim cigarette for women only. New Virginia Slims.

Regular or Menthol.

Virginia Slims are slimmer than the fat cigarettes men smoke. They're tailored slim to fit your hands, your lips, and your purse. And blended with the kind of flavor women like. Rich, mild Virginia flavor. Extra long. Light one up.

You've come a long way.

Sex, American Style

Sex, or at least the idea of it, was suddenly every-where. In June 1969, the sophisticated revue *Oh! Calcutta* provoked controversy when it opened off Broadway, complete with extensive full-frontal nudity and sexually oriented humor by the likes of John Lennon, Sam Shepard, and cartoonist Jules Feiffer. It achieved rave reviews, played to sold-out houses, and ran for 13 years.

With the new ratings system from the Motion Picture Association of America, movies such as **Bob & Carol & Ted & Alice** could now address mature topics. With a tagline of "Consider the possibilities," the film took on the underground suburban phenomenon of wife swapping. Elliott Gould, Natalie Wood, Robert Culp, and Dyan Cannon starred in this Paul Mazursky–directed satire about Eisenhower-era couples trying to become sexually hip.

Television didn't have quite the same latitude, but ABC was game to try with **Love, American Style,** an hour-long comedy with three or four sketches in each show, all of which **dealt with (you guessed it) love in its various permutations.** Each sketch featured a different cast, which at times included Burt Reynolds, Sonny and Cher, Regis Philbin, Martin Sheen, and Mama Cass Elliot. John Astin, Abby Dalton, and George Furth are pictured in this scene.

British soul diva **Dusty Springfield** created her crowning musical statement with *Dusty in Memphis*. This pop/R&B masterpiece, produced by Jerry Wexler, Tom Dowd, and Arif Mardin, flopped upon release and achieved proper "classic" status only in retrospect.

One of rock's most enduringly iconic bands, **Led Zeppelin** became an instant sensation with the release of its eponymous debut album. The group, comprised of former Yardbirds guitarist Jimmy Page, drummer John "Bonzo" Bonham, bassist John Paul Jones, and vocalist Robert Plant, had already perfected a **unique combination of blues classicism, Celtic mythology, and overall power stomp.**

And the Oscar Goes To

1964

Best Picture: *My Fair Lady* ▶

Best Actor: Rex Harrison
  (*My Fair Lady*)

Best Actress: Julie Andrews
  (*Mary Poppins*)

1965

◀ Best Picture: *The Sound of Music*

Best Actor: Lee Marvin (*Cat Ballou*)

Best Actress: Julie Christie (*Darling*)

1966

Best Picture: *A Man for All Seasons*

Best Actor: Paul Scofield (*A Man for All Seasons*)

Best Actress: Elizabeth Taylor (*Who's Afraid of Virginia
  Woolf?*)

1967

Best Picture: *In the Heat of the Night*

Best Actor: Rod Steiger *(In the Heat of the Night)*

Best Actress: Katharine Hepburn
   (Guess Who's Coming to Dinner)

1968

Best Picture: *Oliver!* ▶

Best Actor: Cliff Robertson *(Charly)*

Best Actress: Tie—Katharine
   Hepburn *(The Lion in Winter)*;
   Barbra Streisand *(Funny Girl)*

1969

Best Picture: *Midnight Cowboy*

Best Actor: John Wayne *(True Grit)*

Best Actress: Maggie Smith *(The
   ◀ Prime of Miss Jean Brodie)*

Set in an integrated Los Angeles high school, **_Room 222_** was rare for its time in the manner in which it mixed dramatic elements into a sitcom, regularly addressing such hot-button topics as homophobia, STDs, racism, and teen pregnancy. It starred Lloyd Haynes and Karen Valentine as idealistic teachers, Denise Nicholas as the guidance counselor, and Michael Constantine as the skeptical principal.

A new way of teaching kids through television was created on November 10, 1969, with the launch of *Sesame Street*. Learning became fun with the "spoonful of sugar" approach, employing the fast-paced repetition of advertising and puppets developed by Jim Henson—including Cookie Monster, Bert and Ernie, and Kermit the Frog, who would become the biggest superstar of them all. The show was set in the middle of a New York street, a conscious effort to reach less-educated inner-city children.

Woody Allen's 1969 directorial debut, *Take The Money and Run*—in which he also starred as woefully inefficient criminal Virgil Starkwell—**is still considered a comic gem** for its joke-a-minute script and inventive sight gags (such as the gun carved from soap that foams up in the rain).

America was uniformly stunned at the marriage of bizarre novelty act **Tiny Tim** and his teenage bride, **"Miss Vicky" Budinger.** Their merger took place on December 17, 1969, before Johnny Carson and a **Tonight Show** audience of 45 million, making it the highest-rated single episode of a talk show in TV history.

The '60s dream embodied by Woodstock came crashing down in the nightmare of Altamont. The Rolling Stones wanted to end their American tour with a free concert and at the last minute settled upon this isolated Northern California speedway as the venue. The Hell's Angels motorcycle gang, which had previously served as security for the Grateful Dead without incident, was hired to keep the peace. But on December 9, 1969, everything went haywire: For starters, Jefferson Airplane's Marty Balin, his head bloodied, was knocked unconscious by an Angel. While the Stones themselves were onstage, a young man in the audience was stabbed by Angels and beaten to death with pool cues.

The Lottery No One Wanted to Win

By December 1969, nearly half a million American soldiers were deployed in Vietnam. The draft process that had taken them there, of drafting the oldest first, came to be seen as unfair, and the government established a draft lottery in its place. American males between 18 and 26 years of age would be drafted based on a random drawing. A hopper contained 366 blue plastic capsules, each marked with a different month and day for every possible birth date. In one turn of that hopper, the war suddenly became much more immediate for a large number of people. New York Representative Alexander Pirnie drew the first date, September 14. All men born on that date between 1944 and 1950 were now first in line for the draft. Nearly 600,000 young American men would be drafted before conscription was suspended in June 1973.

Index